WORD DRIVEN
SPIRIT LED

John

Cover design and art work: Donnie Morrison

ISBN-13: 978-0-988403208

ISBN-10: 0-9884032-0-X

Library of Congress Catalog Number 2012922438

Printed in the United States of America

www.WordDrivenSpiritLed.com

DEDICATION

This book is dedicated to my Lord, Savior and Master Jesus Christ who saved me and transformed me into the person I am today. I eagerly look forward to meeting Him face to face when He comes to take His people home.

I thank Him for the Word He has given to me. Nothing in life is more important to me than to treasure, read, memorize, understand and apply His Word in my life daily.

I thank Him for the Holy Spirit who patiently works in my life as He teaches me to apply His Word. He is my spiritual guide as I strive to understand the scriptures and grow in holiness.

This book would not be a reality if it was not for the transforming power of His Word and the trustworthy guidance of His Spirit.

All praise and glory be to His name.

FOR

MY MOM, KAMALA

AND

MY DAD, JAMES

ACKNOWLEDGMENTS

I would like to thank Glenn Hill, friend and senior pastor at Calvary Chapel, Ridgecrest, California, for his review of the initial and final manuscript and his guidance on the content of this book.

I would like to thank Mike Gray, for his review of the initial and final manuscript to ensure biblical accuracy of the content.

I would like to specially thank Rosemary Gilbert for her review and final edit of the manuscript. Without your in-depth review and corrections, this manuscript would not have been completed. Thank you so much.

I would like to thank Donnie Morrison for cover design and art work. Praise God for the talents He has given you.

I would like to thank my wife Anila, for her patience and support while I worked on this book.

I would like to thank my daughters Nasya, Nita and Nysa for proof-reading initial drafts and cross checking references. I also thank my daughters for their understanding during the times I worked on the book instead of hanging out with them. I hope that someday you will read this book and we will have fun discussing it during family gatherings.

ABOUT THE AUTHOR

John Paul is an assistant pastor at Calvary Chapel, Ridgecrest, California and enjoys teaching, counseling, and discipleship as the Lord allows him to, in the ministry of equipping the saints. John is blessed with a wife and four daughters, including twins, and enjoys spending as much time as possible with his family. John's purpose in life is to know Jesus and to make Him known.

John currently works as a technical manager for the Naval Air Warfare Center, located in California. With a Masters in Electrical Engineering, John enjoys working with the latest weapons and avionics technology supporting the United States war-fighter.

CONTENTS

CHAPTER 1

INTRODUCTION

Hebrews 10:25 says that the day is approaching. Never before has this statement become so true than it is today. The Lord is ready to return to rapture His people home. Are you waiting for the Lord? If not, then you are not ready to meet Him face to face.

The world is not helping the situation either. Everywhere you turn you see the world working against Christians. The church also seems to be subtly falling prey to a New World Order that opposes any biblical principle that Christians want to follow.

Look around the world - you can see churches losing their Christian integrity and following the doctrines of the Scripture only when it is convenient. We no longer see the Pauls or Peters of the Bible in today's world. But we do see a lot of Davids who still have not met their Nathans. Even after they encounter their Nathans, they do not seem to realize that Nathan is talking about them. So oblivious to God's direct admonition, they are caught up in the pleasures of the world and of self, and it seems like ultimately, God gives them over to the sinful desires of their hearts. Eventually many end up exchanging the truth of God for a lie. They worship and serve created things rather than the Creator. I am not talking about unbelievers but about born-again Christians who resemble the pagans described in Romans.

> Therefore God also gave them up to uncleanness, in the lusts of their hearts, to dishonor their bodies among themselves, who exchanged the truth of God for the lie, and worshiped and served the creature

rather than the Creator, who is blessed forever. Amen. (Romans 1:24-25)

Churches are giving in to the pressures of the world. Pastors preach watered-down sermons, giving church-goers what they want to hear rather than teaching and admonishing them to comply with God's Word through His strength. Their sermons may quote scriptures but in the end, they only deliver a motivational speech promising God's blessing on everyone without requiring any accountability. There are also outright cultish churches that purposefully lead the congregation away from true fellowship with our sovereign, omnipotent, and ever-loving God.

In this process of transition from the truth to a lie, Satan is actively and subtly leading people astray. With so much new technology and knowledge that provide instant answers to all our questions and instant access to world-wide information, who needs a God that demands uncompromising devotion and allegiance? We seem to have placed God on hold, only calling on Him when there is a need. And we blame God when He does not give us what we want. Satan seems to be gaining an upper hand in his scheme of deception and lies. He is using worldly truths as his powerful weapon. And when this truth is staring at you, why do you need faith? Satan is working from inside the church to deceive God's very elect. It concerns me greatly that the church is turning a deaf ear to the warnings in the Bible.

I was born again in 1973 at the age of thirteen years. Having been born into a Christian family, I knew all about Jesus Christ, son of the Almighty God, who died for me on the cross. But it was not until I hit a road block in my life that I felt the need for a Savior to fill a burning void in my life. Although I gave my life to Christ at the age of thirteen, I did not know how to turn my life around. I asked God to change me, but nothing happened. I tried to change me with my own strength, making promises to God that I could not keep. After many failed attempts at changing my life, I was at a stalemate. The desire to be holy was always there, but the means of achieving any resemblance of holiness escaped me. Many a time I screamed to God, "Change me," but He seemed to be too busy working on other people.

Now after over thirty years of being a born-again Christian, I am still learning to pursue holiness. There are certain principles of spiritual growth that have helped in my spiritual walk with the Lord. While I am far from being perfect, these principles guarantee all Christians the spiritual growth they so passionately desire.

In this short book I wish to present these principles along with two powerful persons that enable you to practically apply the principles in your life. Following them has transformed my life from one of spiritual instability to one of increasing spiritual progress. Diligently applying these principles from the scriptures, the Bible guarantees a supernatural life transformation. You will experience God's touch here on earth and prepare to, one day, meet Him face to face.

> These things I have spoken to you, that My joy may remain in you, and that your joy may be full. (John 15:11)

The first person is the extremely powerful Word of God. I refer to the Word as a person because the Word of God is really Jesus Christ.

> In the beginning was the Word, and the Word was with God, and the Word was God. 2 He was in the beginning with God. (John 1:1)

> And the Word became flesh and dwelt among us, and we beheld His glory, the glory as of the only begotten of the Father, full of grace and truth. (John 1:14)

There is nothing more important in life than to let the Word of God define and drive your everyday activities, no matter whether they are spiritual in nature or otherwise.

The second person is the Holy Spirit, who is our guide and spiritual leader. But He can only lead if we submit to Him.

> Therefore, brethren, we are debtors — not to the flesh, to live according to the flesh. For if you live according to the flesh you will die; but if by the Spirit you put to death the deeds of the body, you will live. For as many as are led by the Spirit of God, these are sons of God. (Romans 8:12-14)

> If we live in the Spirit, let us also walk in the Spirit. (Galatians 5:25)

> And do not be drunk with wine, in which is dissipation; but be filled with the Spirit. (Ephesians 5:18)

Being filled with the Spirit is equivalent to submitting ourselves to the guidance of the Holy Spirit.

Your life has to be "*Word Driven*" and "*Spirit Led*" to experience the changed life that is promised to every born-again Christian.

> Therefore, if anyone is in Christ, he is a new creation; old things have passed away; behold, all things have become new. (2 Corinthians 5:17)

How much of your life has become new since you were born again? To measure the change, you need a standard. This standard is given to us in Ephesians 5.

> Therefore be imitators of God as dear children. And walk in love, as Christ also has loved us and given Himself for us, an offering and a sacrifice to God for a sweet-smelling aroma. (Ephesians 5:1-2)

To be imitators of God is no small task and requires diligent action on our part. Paul describes the radical change required of every born-again believer in Galatians. Here, the acts of the sinful nature contrast the fruit of the Spirit. Note the singularity of the Spirit's fruit.

> Now the works of the flesh are evident, which are: adultery, fornication, uncleanness, lewdness, idolatry, sorcery, hatred, contentions, jealousies, outbursts of wrath, selfish ambitions, dissensions, heresies, envy, murders, drunkenness, revelries, and the like; of which I tell you beforehand, just as I also told you in time past, that those who practice such things will not inherit the kingdom of God. But the fruit of the Spirit is love, joy, peace, longsuffering, kindness, goodness, faithfulness, gentleness, self-control. Against such there is no law. (Galatians 5:19-23)

This change is sought after by many a believer but seldom realized. This book shows you how to be "*Word Driven*" and "*Spirit Led*" so you may be "partakers of the divine nature" that Paul describes.

> Grace and peace be multiplied to you in the knowledge of God and of Jesus our Lord, as His divine power has given to us all things that pertain to life and godliness, through the knowledge of Him who called us by glory and virtue, by which have been

15

given to us exceedingly great and precious promises, that through these you may be *partakers of the divine nature*, having escaped the corruption that is in the world through lust. (2 Peter 1:2-4)

In the Department of Defense, where I currently work, every product that is delivered to the war-fighter is verified and validated for compliance to the product's requirements. That activity is called "verification and validation" and consists of lots of product testing. In the same way, I urge you to verify, validate, and test every principle that I present to you in this book. Filter it through the infallible Word of God to ensure the strictest compliance with God's truth revealed to us in His beautiful scriptures.

Our God Almighty wants a holy nation, not a big nation. As much grace as He pours out on us, we should not use it to continue in sin. We must seek to be holy with a deep passion that translates biblical principles into practical applications for our everyday lives.

> I beseech you therefore, brethren, by the mercies of God, that you present your bodies a living sacrifice, holy, acceptable to God, which is your reasonable service. And do not be conformed to this world, but be transformed by the renewing of your mind, that you may prove what is that good and acceptable and perfect will of God. (Romans 12:1-2)

May the Lord Himself transform your life as you understand the principles and study the scriptures presented in this book.

CHAPTER 1

PERSONAL

NOTES

CHAPTER 2

THE LAW

OF

HUMAN NATURE

Every time I read Romans, it reminds me of the struggle that Paul describes. He has a problem and is not afraid to confess it to the world. He realizes that confessing his weakness is not a sign of a spiritual wimp but one of a spiritual need. It is the need for a supernatural power that brings about the transformation he desires.

> I find then a law, that evil is present with me, the one who wills to do good. For I delight in the law of God according to the inward man. But I see another law in my members, warring against the law of my mind, and bringing me into captivity to the law of sin which is in my members. O wretched man that I am! Who will deliver me from this body of death? I thank God — through Jesus Christ our Lord!   (Romans 7:21-25)

For us to understand the law that works in every born-again Christian, we need to revisit Adam and Eve in the Garden of Eden.

The Scriptures state that God created Adam and Eve in His own image. This image refers to His character and not to a physical image because God is spirit as recorded in John 4:24. God then gave them authority over everything else created.

He also gave them permission to eat of every fruit in the garden, except from the tree of the knowledge of good and evil (Genesis 2:15).

We know that Adam and Eve sinned and got separated from God when Satan deceived them. What we may not know or see is the process that Satan used to deceive the very children of God who were in the very image of God. One would think that being Holy and in the very image of God is good enough to overcome Satan's temptations, but it is not. This thought leads to a very important principle - free choice. No matter what the state of your spiritual growth or how many victories you have had in your spiritual warfare, you must always be on guard to make choices that comply with God's Word. Holiness is a result of our uncompromising devotion and love for God and not an automatic change resulting from our salvation by grace through faith.

Satan in his original created form was one of the most beautiful angels God created. In fact, Satan was God's confidant who enjoyed being part of daily discussions and the decision-making process in God's presence. Nevertheless God gave Satan the free choice of either continuing to be under His authority or giving in to prideful behavior.

> How you are fallen from heaven, O Lucifer, son of
> the morning!
> How you are cut down to the ground,
> You who weakened the nations!
> For you have said in your heart:
> 'I will ascend into heaven,
> I will exalt my throne above the stars of God;
> I will also sit on the mount of the congregation
> On the farthest sides of the north;

I will ascend above the heights of the clouds,
I will be like the Most High.'
Yet you shall be brought down to Sheol,
To the lowest depths of the Pit. (Isaiah 14:12-15)

Satan, also known as Lucifer wants to be God, even though he was what one could refer to as a "good" angel. Even though Lucifer had a very close relationship with God, he chose to give in to his pride.

So in the Garden of Eden, Satan knew that once he presents a choice to Eve, he stood a chance that Eve would disobey God. This choice is a chance for her and Adam to become like God. Let us briefly look at Satan's strategy as he deceived Eve. Note that his strategy has not changed since the Garden of Eden. Perhaps you will see what a familiar situation it is even today.

> Now the serpent was more cunning than any beast of the field which the Lord God had made. And he said to the woman, "Has God indeed said, 'You shall not eat of every tree of the garden'?" (Genesis 3:1)

Satan uses the very Word of God, meaning God's command to Adam and Eve, as he starts the conversation with Eve. Also note that Eve might not have known about Satan and his prior role as Lucifer in the heavenly kingdom of God. I believe that God did not reveal the nature or existence of Satan to Adam and Eve. He wanted them to obey Him for the sole reason of their love and devotion to Him, not because they did not want to give in to Satan. I also believe that God continues to operate with us on the same principle. He wants us to love Him of our own free will, not because something bad will happen to us if we disobey Him. We need to get to that state in our spiritual life that we love and obey God not because we have to but because we want to.

Eve rightly responds to Satan when he challenged the accuracy of the Word of God. She repeated what God has commanded them to do regarding the tree of the knowledge of good and evil.

Satan immediately disagrees and explains that God did not want them to eat the fruit. He states that if they did they would be like God Himself, knowing what is good and what is evil. We again see Satan's character here as he tries to convince Eve to do exactly what he did – free choice. Eve now thinks that being like God, knowing the difference between good and evil is perhaps a good thing. The next verse is very important to understand the nature of humans from the perspective of their sinful nature. In Gen 3:6, Eve demonstrates that every human, even one who closely walks with God, is susceptible to sin. Let us examine this verse in detail.

> So when the woman saw that the tree was good for food, that it was pleasant to the eyes, and a tree desirable to make one wise, she took of its fruit and ate. She also gave to her husband with her, and he ate. (Genesis 3:6)

In this verse, God reveals to us the three general types of sin that a human being is susceptible to.

a.) Eve saw that the tree was good for food.
b.) Eve realized that it was pleasant to the eyes.
c.) Eve was convinced that it would make her wise.

Every sin falls into one of these categories. Let us compare what Eve did here to a scripture in 1 John.

> Do not love the world or the things in the world. If anyone loves the world, the love of the Father is not in him. For all that is in the world — the lust of the flesh, the lust of the eyes, and the pride of life — is not of the Father but is of the world. (1 John 2:15-16)

Here God shows us that sin is classified into three types.

    a.) Lust of the flesh.
    b.) Lust of the eyes.
    c.) The pride of life.

There is a direct correlation between what Eve did and what God tells us in 1 John 2:15-16.

Realizing that the tree was good for food, Eve demonstrates our susceptibility to the lust of the flesh. Seeing that the tree was pleasant to the eyes, Eve demonstrates our susceptibility to the lust of the eyes. Believing that the tree would make her wise and like God, Eve demonstrates our susceptibility to the pride of life.

Eve proves to us that all human nature is susceptible to sin. But God proves to us that through Jesus Christ it is quite possible to resist Satan and his deceptive ways of alluring us to sin.

Let us now examine the temptation of Jesus Christ. Just like Eve faced the temptation of Satan in the Garden of Eden, Jesus Christ faced the devil in the wilderness. We read about this temptation in Matthew 4. Go ahead and open your Bible and read the first 11 verses of Matthew 4. Let me point out something in the very first verse.

> Then Jesus was led up by the Spirit into the wilderness to be tempted by the devil. (Matthew 4:1)

The Holy Spirit leads Jesus to be tempted by the devil. Here is the first occurrence of spiritual warfare into which Jesus was led by the Holy Spirit and prevailed. We see that He had not eaten anything for forty days and forty nights. He was in His weakest physical form. Nevertheless, He prevailed and His responses in verses 4, 7, and 10 reveal His strategy for spiritual war. It was driven by the Word of God.

Ever wonder why The Holy Spirit led Jesus into a spiritual conflict with the devil when He was physically weak? It is to show us through Jesus' example that spiritual warfare can be won if and only if we are *Word Driven* and *Spirit Led*.

Jesus fasted for forty days and forty nights and was very hungry. He was probably ready for a juicy sirloin steak with all the trimmings, a succulent side of vegetables, and a triple fudge ice cream sundae. Here comes Satan knowing Jesus' state of extreme hunger. Satan tempts Jesus asking Him to use His power to change the stones to bread. In other words, Satan challenges Jesus – "You can work miracles. Why don't you prove it to me and make yourself some bread and feed your hunger?" Does this sound familiar? Satan tempts Jesus with the *lust of the flesh*. But Jesus resists.

Next, Satan takes Jesus to the holy city, Jerusalem, and sits Him on top of the pinnacle of the temple. Satan then proceeds to challenge Jesus again to throw himself down because God will send His angels to protect him. In other words, Satan challenges Jesus – "You are invincible. Why don't you prove it to me by throwing yourself down to die?" Does this sound familiar? Satan tempts Jesus with the *pride of life*. But Jesus resists.

Next, Satan takes Jesus to a high mountain and shows him the whole world. Satan then presents a proposal. "Look Jesus, you came to set this world free from me. I will give this world to you, everything you see will be yours, and I will leave you and the world forever, if you just worship me once." Does this sound familiar again? Satan tempts Jesus with the *lust of the eyes*. But Jesus resists.

Contrast this temptation with that in the Garden of Eden. The first Adam, through Eve, did not resist Satan and through that sin affected the future of the next generations, until Jesus Christ. The second Adam, Jesus Christ, who was *Word Driven* and *Spirit Led*, resisted Satan and through that victory affected the future all of those who believed on Him.

Now relating the temptation of Jesus Christ and the temptation of Eve with the caution that God gives to us in 1 John 2:15-16, we see that there are three types or classifications of sin. We also see that Eve demonstrates that every human being is susceptible to every kind of sin. Fortunately, we also see that Jesus demonstrates that every born-again believer is now capable of resisting every kind of sin.

No matter where you are in your personal walk with the Lord, whether you are just a Christian baby or a Christian adult, the susceptibility to sin has never changed since the creation. This susceptibility to sin is the law of human nature.

Although when born-again, a person is freed from the *penalty of sin*, a believer is never free from the *power of sin* until we get to heaven. Freedom from this law of human nature comes only from being *Word Driven* and *Spirit Led*.

CHAPTER 2

PERSONAL

NOTES

CHAPTER 3

THE BEGINNING

OF

HOLINESS

In Chapter 2, we saw how Adam and Eve yielded to Satan's temptation by eating of the fruit from the tree of knowledge of good and evil.

One might wonder about the significance of the tree of knowledge of good and evil. Let me present to you a conversation I had with a young lady, about the time I was writing this book. I was on a business trip to Honolulu, HI for meetings with the U.S. Fleet Forces, Pacific Command. Having finished for the day a little early, my colleagues and I decided to grab a bite to eat in Waikiki Beach. One of my colleagues was a sweet young lady, who is also an excellent engineer. Between conversations about work and fun activities in Waikiki, our talk turned towards the topic of religion. As with any opportunity that presents itself to me, I started to present the gospel gently. I had no prior knowledge of whether my colleagues were born-again Christians or not. I quickly came to know that this young lady, Christine (name changed), used to go to church and was raised Catholic. As I presented her the gospel, I mentioned that being "born-again" was the only sure way of meeting our God in heaven. She then asked me about all the people who are not born-again, and I could tell that my answer suddenly caused her great concern. She asked me, "What if I believe with all my heart that I am doing everything to please God to the best of my ability, and I did not become born-again because of my ignorance? Would God really send me to hell because I was ignorant?"

Christine makes a good point. This point is where the tree of the knowledge of good and evil comes into play. When Adam and Eve ate of the fruit from the tree, they became like God, not in His character but in His knowledge of good and evil. Satan knew this, but Eve must have thought eating the fruit would make her like God in His character. What ended up happening was man became aware of the difference between good and evil. We call this conscience. This first sinful act of disobedience is the reason everyone has this conscience. Not only did man become sinful in nature, he also ended up with something that constantly judged him about the choices he would make from then on.

> Then the Lord God said, "Behold, the man has become like one of Us, to know good and evil."
> (Genesis 3:22)

Let me present this from a different angle. God made Adam and Eve, placed them in the Garden of Eden and said, "Go play." He said, "You can do anything you want. You cannot do anything wrong because you do not know what is wrong." Wow. Imagine the freedom to do whatever you want with no consequences, no guilt, and no punishment. This was possible because neither Adam nor Eve knew the difference between good and evil. Anything they wanted to do was okay with God, except one thing – the commandment from God not to eat of the tree of knowledge of good and evil. There was only one restriction from God that presented them a choice, and they messed it up.

Returning back to the conversation with my colleague, Christine, I did give her an answer. I presented to her the evidences that Jesus indeed was a historical figure. I also presented to her the mathematical impossibility of all the Old Testament prophesies coming true. I explained to her that the Word of God presents to us an indisputable approach for the created being to meet his or her Creator in a personal way. Additionally, I presented to her the fact that because everyone is born with a conscience, all humanity knows they have fallen short of "some" standard, whatever that standard might be. And because of this fundamental aspect of every human being, one cannot claim to be ignorant of failing to meet God's requirements of going to heaven. Given today's technology, the media and the internet, the Christian faith is publicly discussed everywhere. Even films and TV shows present the gospel in one fashion or another. For example, during this same trip to Honolulu, I actually watched an episode of *JAG*, the TV show, where a general is accused of disrupting the war on terror because of his Christian faith.

The knowledge of good and evil presents daily choices for us. If one's conscience stayed pure, as before Adam and Eve ate of the fruit, man could be fairly judged solely on the basis of his conscience.

> Now the Spirit expressly says that in latter times some will depart from the faith, giving heed to deceiving spirits and doctrines of demons, speaking lies in hypocrisy, having their own conscience seared with a hot iron. (1 Timothy 4:1-2)

But the problem is that a conscience can be molded into believing that bad is really something good. This results in a different standard based on how pure one's conscience is.

> To the pure all things are pure, but to those who are defiled and unbelieving nothing is pure; but even their mind and conscience are defiled. (Titus 1:15)

So God came up with a standard to avoid any confusion. He laid down the law in the Ten Commandments which He knew no one could follow. He holds us accountable to this uniform standard so we can see how sinful we are. Just as a conscience shows us good versus evil, the Ten Commandments show us what we must comply with to be considered God's people. And because everyone has fallen short, the law shows us how sinful the human race is.

> What shall we say then? Is the law sin? Certainly not! On the contrary, I would not have known sin except through the law. For I would not have known covetousness unless the law had said, "You shall not covet." But sin, taking opportunity by the commandment, produced in me all manner of evil desire. For apart from the law sin was dead. (Romans 7:7-8)

Then God created the wonderful plan of salvation and made it available to anyone who believes in Jesus Christ as his or her Savior.

> For by grace you have been saved through faith, and that not of yourselves; it is the gift of God, not of works, lest anyone should boast. For we are His workmanship, created in Christ Jesus for good works,

which God prepared beforehand that we should walk in them. (Ephesians 2:8-10)

God gave this salvation to everyone completely apart from the law. What the law was unable to accomplish, God accomplished through His Son Jesus Christ.

> For the law of the Spirit of life in Christ Jesus has made me free from the law of sin and death. For what the law could not do in that it was weak through the flesh, God did by sending His own Son in the likeness of sinful flesh, on account of sin: He condemned sin in the flesh, that the righteous requirement of the law might be fulfilled in us who do not walk according to the flesh but according to the Spirit. For those who live according to the flesh set their minds on the things of the flesh, but those who live according to the Spirit, the things of the Spirit. (Romans 8:2-5)

This plan of salvation was made available not just to the Jews, the chosen race of God, but to everyone who believes in the Lord Jesus Christ. Salvation is not based on the covenant that God made with Abraham, but on the sacrifice of Jesus Christ, who is a propitiation for the entire world.

> But now the righteousness of God apart from the law is revealed, being witnessed by the Law and the Prophets, even the righteousness of God, through faith in Jesus Christ, to all and on all who believe. (Romans 3:21-22)

Propitiation is the process by which God forgives a sinner unconditionally and remains within His Godly character. Jesus Christ achieved this forgiveness through His perfect sacrifice. This salvation is not based on either the law or the works. It is not dependant on our lifestyle. Salvation rests solely on a person's belief that Jesus Christ paid the penalty for the human race once and for all on the cross. His precious blood was offered as the perfect sacrifice for the whole world. Salvation is also not dependant on the state of one's conscience, no matter how defiled it is.

> Previously saying, "Sacrifice and offering, burnt offerings, and offerings for sin You did not desire, nor had pleasure in them"(which are offered according to the law), then He said, "Behold, I have come to do Your will, O God." He takes away the first that He may establish the second. By that will we have been sanctified through the offering of the body of Jesus Christ once for all. (Hebrews 10:8-10)

If you are reading this chapter and have doubts about your own salvation, may I present to you the simple salvation plan that Jesus gave you as a free gift?

> Principle #1 – Romans 3:23 says, "all have sinned and come short of the glory of God." What this means is that irrespective of how good you are, whether you have ever done anything wrong or not, you are still considered short of the standard that God requires of a person to enter into His kingdom.

> Principle #2 – Romans 6:23 says, "the wages of sin is death but the gift of God is eternal life." Many know and have memorized John 3:16 which states that "God so loved the world that he gave his only begotten son, that whosoever believes in Him shall

not perish but have everlasting life." God offered His son Jesus Christ to pay the penalty of your sins so that you can have eternal life in heaven.

Principle #3 – Hebrews 9:27 says, "as it is appointed unto man once to die and after this the judgment." You have one chance, perhaps today is that chance, to believe in Jesus Christ as your savior. Your status of salvation is sealed once and for all when you die. The decision has to be made before your life on earth ends. The decision is yours and yours alone, and you do not lose anything by giving your life to God.

Principle #4 – Revelation 3:20 says, "Behold, I stand at the door and knock. If anyone hears My voice and opens the door, I will come in to him and dine with him, and he with Me." Jesus Christ is inviting you to become part of His kingdom. If you accept Him, you become a child of God and have access to his immense spiritual wealth through a personal relationship with Him. Christianity is not a religion but a relationship with Jesus Christ.

If you do want to believe in Jesus and accept Him as your Savior, here is a simple prayer that must be offered with both sincerity of heart and willingness to accept His sacrifice as a free gift.

> Lord Jesus, I want to become a born-again Christian. I believe you died for me on the cross. I am a sinner, and I need you to save me from my sin. I accept you as my savior and ask you to forgive my sins that I have

committed in my life. Please forgive me and accept me as your child. I commit my life into your hands and ask for your help as I live my life from now on for your glory. In Jesus name, Amen.

Principle #5 – John 1:12 says, "But as many as received Him, to them He gave the right to become children of God, to those who believe in His name."

If you have believed and prayed that prayer, let me be the first to congratulate you and welcome you into the vast kingdom of God's people. I strongly urge you to let another believer know about your salvation. Find a Calvary Chapel or another Bible teaching church to attend so you can fellowship with other believers.

Now that Jesus Christ has accomplished his perfect plan of salvation in every born-again believer, it is ours forever. By doing this, Jesus set us free once and for all from the penalty of sin.

Along with salvation, He also did something vital to the conscience that many do not realize.

For if the blood of bulls and goats and the ashes of a heifer, sprinkling the unclean, sanctifies for the purifying of the flesh, how much more shall the blood of Christ, who through the eternal Spirit offered Himself without spot to God, cleanse your conscience from dead works to serve the living God? (Hebrews 9:13-14)

The same sacrifice on the cross also erases the conscience

from the corruption caused by our sinful nature. Because the conscience is now purged, cleansed, and erased, we can now reprogram it with a newer standard that comes from God through His Word. This new standard opens the door for the Holy Spirit to transform a Christian into the likeness of Jesus Christ.

Being saved is not the end; it is just the beginning of a lifelong relationship between the created being and the Creator. During this relationship, God wants to restore the created being to his or her original state of creation, that is to His own image in which Adam and Eve were created.

This transformation into the image of God is what we refer to as becoming holy and is accomplished by no strategy other than *"Word Driven, Sprit Led."*

CHAPTER 3

PERSONAL

NOTES

CHAPTER 4

THE HEART

AND

THE MIND

Jesus Christ explains in Matthew that we must love Him with our intellectual faculties that govern our choices and convictions.

> Jesus said to him, "You shall love the Lord your God with all your heart, with all your soul, and with all your mind." (Matthew 22:37)

The heart, soul and mind refer to three distinct faculties of our intellectual being. The soul is what leaves the physical body when one perishes. The soul either goes to heaven or is sent to hell for eternity. The soul is what defines the person, the personality and the individual nature that God has given to a human being. Most important to note is that the soul spends eternity with either Jesus in heaven or with Satan in hell.

> And do not fear those who kill the body but cannot kill the soul. But rather fear Him who is able to destroy both soul and body in hell. (Matthew 10:28)

> For what will it profit a man if he gains the whole world, and loses his own soul? (Mark 8:36)

But we need to understand that the soul becomes what the

mind and the heart influence it to be. The heart is the faculty that is the central seat of emotional expression for a human being. In addition, it drives ones actions, whether good or evil. It is described as inherently evil.

> The heart is deceitful above all things, And desperately wicked; Who can know it? (Jeremiah 17:9)

> For out of the heart proceed evil thoughts, murders, adulteries, fornications, thefts, false witness, blasphemies. (Matthew 15:19)

Look at the command that God gave to Israel in the Old Testament.

> Hear, O Israel: The Lord our God, the Lord is one! You shall love the Lord your God with all your heart, with all your soul, and with all your strength. And these words which I command you today shall be in your heart. You shall teach them diligently to your children, and shall talk of them when you sit in your house, when you walk by the way, when you lie down, and when you rise up. You shall bind them as a sign on your hand, and they shall be as frontlets between your eyes. You shall write them on the doorposts of your house and on your gates. (Deuteronomy 6:4-9)

This same commandment is repeated in the New Testament (Matthew 22:37) and the heart comes first in both verses, one from Yahweh and one from Jesus. In Deuteronomy 6:4 God requires that these commands must be stored in the heart which greatly influences the soul and defines a person's character. As an organ in the physical body, the heart is central for the person to be alive. If a person is unhealthy or injured, other organs allow time for diagnosis and treatment. But if the heart stops beating, it can be the end of life. My mother, who God blessed with a full life, died at eighty four due to a heart attack. When the heart stops beating it stops pumping blood and oxygen to the rest of the body, thus affecting the entire body. Similarly, the spiritual heart is vital for the spiritual being and defines the moral and spiritual character of the soul. It is in the heart that convictions are made.

The mind is the faculty that defines a human being's ability to think, understand, reason, and make decisions. As discussed in Chapter 3, the conscience helps distinguish between good and evil. The reference to conscience in several New Testament books could perhaps indicate that the mind also includes this conscience. One of the references is

> Now the purpose of the commandment is love from
> a pure heart, from a good conscience, and from
> sincere faith. (1 Timothy 1:5)

I would describe the conscience as memory which comes with the basic knowledge of good and evil. The mind goes to this memory frequently to get what is currently stored in it as good and evil. Every person is born with this conscience programmed with the knowledge of good and evil, but not everyone is born with the same standard definition of good and evil. Hence the differences in the moral character of human beings. Even though everyone is born with a unique conscience, it can be erased and reprogrammed to have the same standard data for making decisions about good and evil. It is in the mind that decisions to act are made based on the information contained in the conscience.

Born-again believers face a couple of basic problems: the disparity between the mind and the heart, and the disparity between the conscience and the decision making process in the mind. With so much knowledge out on the World Wide Web (WWW), it is hard to trust your own self, your friends, your family or even your pastor to decide what is good or evil. There is only one who is qualified to look into your heart and mind.

> I, the Lord, search the heart, I test the mind, Even to give every man according to his ways, According to the fruit of his doings. (Jeremiah 17:10)

Allow God to get into your heart and mind to align the two so decisions made in the mind comply with the convictions made in the heart.

There are two activities that must happen to facilitate the transformation.

The first is the renewal of the mind. By reprogramming of the conscience every believer is governed by a standard set of rules defining good and evil.

> I beseech you therefore, brethren, by the mercies of God, that you present your bodies a living sacrifice, holy, acceptable to God, which is your reasonable service. And do not be conformed to this world, but be transformed by the *renewing of your mind*, that you may prove what is that good and acceptable and perfect will of God. (Romans 12:1-2)

The renewing of the mind is the reprogramming of the conscience in our mind. The data that it was born with or programmed with during your life as an unbeliever must be first erased and then written over with the new standard that the Bible defines for us.

The blood of Jesus Christ erases the conscience as discussed in Chapter 3. But every born-again believer must reprogram his or her conscience with new data.

The second activity is to drive out the impurities in the heart and make the heart pure and flexible enough that God can change it with the right convictions. The corrupt nature of the heart is clearly described in the Scriptures.

- Jeremiah 17:9 reveals a desperately wicked heart.
- Exodus 4:21 reveals a hardened heart.
- Proverbs 11:20 reveals a perverted heart.
- Job 36:13 shows a heart lacking in God's desire.
- Matthew 15:19-20 states that a heart defiles the person.

As you renew the mind, you must renew the heart as described for us in Ezekiel 11.

> Then I will give them one heart, and I will put a new spirit within them, and take the stony heart out of their flesh, and give them a heart of flesh, that they may walk in My statutes and keep My judgments and do them; and they shall be My people, and I will be their God. (Ezekiel 11:19-20)

God purposes that the heart and the mind must both be renewed so the mind that reasons is brought into compliance with the heart the Lord convicts.

But this is the covenant that I will make with the
house of Israel after those days, says the Lord: I will
put My law in their minds, and write it on their hearts;
and I will be their God, and they shall be My people.
(Jeremiah 31:33)

The same law must be in both the mind and the heart
bringing them into alignment with each other. Once that
alignment happens it is easy for a believer to follow through
with spiritual commitments to God.

There is another reason God requires compliance between
the mind and the heart.

Now the purpose of the commandment is love from
a pure heart, from a good conscience, and from
sincere faith. (1 Timothy 1:5)

1 Timothy 1:5 shows a tight relationship between the heart
and the mind. Here Paul describes the principle of love that
pleases God. It comes from a pure heart and a good
conscience (mind). We achieve this mind-heart compliance by
faith that God can bring this to completion in a born-again
believer. When the mind complies with the heart, it results in
the beautiful product of love that God demands in
Deuteronomy 6:4 and Jesus restates in Matthew 22:37

The renewing of the mind and the heart happens like this.
Feeding on the Word of God by reading and memorizing the
scriptures, the believer renews the mind. The Holy Spirit then
takes the Word of God that is now in the mind and uses that
to renew the heart as the believer submits to His direction.

Note that this change is a continuous change resulting in

increasing holiness in the believer. This change is what Paul refers to as "working out your own salvation."

> Therefore, my beloved, as you have always obeyed, not as in my presence only, but now much more in my absence, work out your own salvation with fear and trembling. (Philippians 2:12)

While the Word renews the mind, the Holy Spirit renews the heart. A believer requires both changes to become and be holy and accomplishes these changes by being *Word Driven* and *Spirit Led.*

CHAPTER 4

PERSONAL

NOTES

CHAPTER 5

THE POWER

OF

GOD'S WORD

In this chapter I want to introduce to you the first of two persons that will change your life forever. That person is the Word of God. I refer to the Word as a person because of John 1:1.

> In the beginning was the Word, and the Word was with God, and the Word was God. (John 1:1)

Anyone who has done an in-depth study of this scripture realizes that Word can be replaced with Jesus without changing the meaning of the verse. John 1:14 also convinces you that the Word personified refers to Jesus Christ.

> And the Word became flesh and dwelt among us, and we beheld His glory, the glory as of the only begotten of the Father, full of grace and truth. (John 1:14)

As an assistant pastor in my church I consistently encourage, admonish and challenge the congregation to be diligent in their Quiet Time (QT) which consists of reading the Word of God and spending time in prayer. This practice of QT is how we build a relationship with God through His Son Jesus Christ.

For example, you invite a guest into your house and have him

47

or her sit in the living room. If you go about doing your normal chores in the house, what good does it do to have a guest? If you were invited to a friend's house and were left by yourself in the living room, would you not be offended? As a believer, you have invited Jesus Christ into your heart. But if you do not make an effort to spend time with Him, how do you think Jesus would feel? Has he been asking you, "My child, why did you invite me into your life if you were not going to spend any time with me?" Maybe it is time to pay attention to that prompting in your heart and make some time to be with the Lord Jesus Christ.

Many believers who have been born again for years still struggle with keeping their QT appointment with Jesus. In this chapter, I will present to you scriptural evidence of the desperate need for God's Word. You cannot accomplish the required transformation without pouring into the Word of God.

In 2006, a product called, "My Therapy Buddy" was introduced on national TV. Its purpose was to help people with depression or anxiety by repeating its signature phrase - "Everything is going to be alright." People carried the therapy buddy around in their house and sometimes outside. Any time they needed encouragement one simple squeeze would repeat those soothing words. The inventor whole heartedly believed that the Therapy Buddy was the answer to people's sadness. I believe that many believers carry the Bible around like the Therapy Buddy. They will only open it when they need to hear something soothing, something that will put their heart and mind at ease. Once they feel better, the Bible goes back on the desk or on the mantle or back in the book case in the study.

My dear brothers and sisters, it is time to go past the point of just being saved and start building a relationship with Jesus. Only then can you can see His power demonstrated in your life. For me, it has been the craziest of an adrenaline filled roller coaster ride since I started having my QT regularly. Not just to put a check mark in my daily routine, but to seriously consider His teachings and make a personal and practical application in my life. It is not magic that just happens; it is the Word of God that transforms your mind through its sanctifying power.

> Sanctify them by Your truth. Your word is truth.
> (John 17:17)

I believe the transformation needed in every believer is primarily based on the quantity and quality of time you invest into the Word of God. The Bible is very clear as it describes the importance of the Word of God in our lives. Let us look at Joshua 1:8 again.

> This Book of the Law shall not depart from your mouth, but you shall meditate in it day and night, that you may observe to do according to all that is written in it. For then you will make your way prosperous, and then you will have good success. (Joshua 1:8)

In this scripture, there are three things that the Lord commands Joshua to do: read the Bible, think about what you have read, and then diligently make a practical application in your life. When you do that, you will be prosperous and successful. Success and prosperity are a result of these three actions that you take with respect to the Word of God.

So how does the Word of God accomplish this most sought

after result when you read, think and apply the Word of God? Let us look at 2 Timothy 3:16-17.

> All Scripture is given by inspiration of God, and is profitable for *doctrine*, for *reproof*, for *correction*, for *instruction in righteousness*, that the man of God may be complete, thoroughly equipped for every good work. (2 Timothy 3:16-17)

Examining this scripture, you can see there are four instances of why God's Word is profitable for us. I see our walk with the Lord as a spiritual highway. I call it The Highway of Holiness.

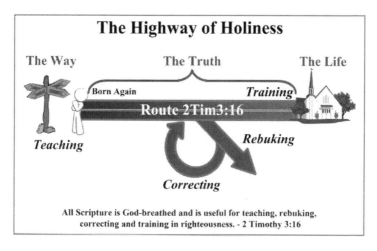

The Highway of Holiness

The Way   The Truth   The Life

Born Again   Training

Route 2Tim3:16

Teaching   *Rebuking*

Correcting

All Scripture is God-breathed and is useful for teaching, rebuking, correcting and training in righteousness. - 2 Timothy 3:16

First, God's Word tells us how to get on the highway by explaining to us biblical *doctrines* that we need to accept. Second, driving on this spiritual highway, we see many distractions, some caused by our own foolishness and some that Satan brings our way. When that happens, we go off the spiritual highway and God's Word tells us that we got off at the wrong exit. This is God's *reproof*. When we take the wrong exit, we need to know how to get back on the highway. God's

Word shows us how to carefully navigate ourselves back on the highway. This is God's *correction*. The fourth instance where God's Word is profitable to us is the *instruction* it provides to live a righteous life. God's Word shows us how we can stay on the spiritual highway. Staying on the spiritual highway requires the renewing of the mind and the transformation of the heart.

To have a desire for the Word we must first believe in its authenticity. Many will question the validity and human aspect of error when it comes to the Bible. They won't question the theories of science but will question if the Word of God is true. Ever wonder why that is? It is because science presents to us the things that the mind reasons as a practical possibility. What the Bible presents is a practical impossibility that the mind cannot reason as acceptable. How can one go to heaven by just believing in Jesus that no one has seen for 2000 years? How can God create something out of nothing? How can Jesus die a normal death and come back to life? These are aspects of spirituality that don't depend on your feelings or your understanding. These require faith in the invisible God and His power through His Word.

If we do not believe that the Bible is actually the spoken Word of God, we will not experience the change that the Word can bring about in our personal life. In the next few chapters, we will see why the Bible is authoritative, authentic, God-spoken Word that has the power to change you. There are many scriptures throughout the Bible that we can examine, but I have chosen Psalm 19:7-11 for this purpose.

> The law of the Lord is perfect, converting the soul;
> The testimony of the Lord is sure, making wise the

simple;
The statutes of the Lord are right, rejoicing the heart;
The commandment of the Lord is pure, enlightening
the eyes;
The fear of the Lord is clean, enduring forever;
The judgments of the Lord are true and righteous
altogether.
More to be desired are they than gold, Yea, than
much fine gold;
Sweeter also than honey and the honeycomb.
Moreover by them Your servant is warned,
And in keeping them there is great reward.
(Psalm 19:7-11)

There are several aspects of God's Word that David, the
Psalmist, understood and documented for us in Psalms. Let
us focus in and examine the four characteristics of God's
Word stated in verses 7 and 8. In the next few chapters we
will understand what it means to be *Word Driven*.

CHAPTER 5

PERSONAL

NOTES

CHAPTER 6

GOD'S WORD

IS

PERFECT

In this chapter we will examine the first and very important characteristic of God's Word that David the Psalmist documented for us.

> The law of the Lord is *perfect*, converting the soul. (Psalm 19:7a)

My work with the Department of Defense involves developing and deploying systems to our military forces around the world. These systems are required to work when needed. If something goes wrong, it is the design engineer that is called to investigate, explain and then come up with a suitable fix. In the medical field, when something is seriously wrong with a person, we call the specialists. My sister is a specialist in anesthesiology and is called in for cases that are very critical in nature. She knows exactly how much anesthesia to administer for a particular case, and she is very good at it. We always look to the experts when things need fixing. In the same way, if we need fixing for our spiritual body, we must go to the expert who created it. We must ask this expert to fix the issue. In the technical world we call these experts Subject Matter Experts or SMEs. Our Almighty God is the SME when it comes to matters related to the heart and mind. When He speaks, His words are perfect, meaning that His advice is complete and has no discrepancies. Let us look at another scripture to help us understand the validity of God's Word.

> Knowing this first, that no prophecy of Scripture is of any private interpretation, for prophecy never came by the will of man, but holy men of God spoke as they were moved by the Holy Spirit. (2 Peter 1:20-21)

We must believe that people did not write the Bible because they wanted to. God inspired them through His Holy Spirit to document history as well as prophecy. Sometimes this history was not part of their lives but was revealed to them by the Holy Spirit. Consider the fact that the Bible was written by forty different authors over a span of 1600 years. Yet the central theme of the Bible - Jesus and His free gift of salvation - has been preserved throughout the ages and throughout the Bible. That mathematically impossible achievement is possible only if the same person guided all forty different authors. Many modern day scholars discredit the Bible as the authentic Word of God and point out the mistakes or inconsistencies. Perhaps there are areas that we do not fully understand or seem to be inconsistent. These challenging areas do not change the message that is engrained into the content.

Consider this also. There are so many messianic prophecies in the Old Testament that are fulfilled in Jesus Christ. Let us look at the probability of one prophecy. In 700 B.C the prophet Micah prophesied in Micah 5:2 that the tiny village of Bethlehem would be the birthplace of Jesus Christ. The fact that Jesus was born in Bethlehem is one of the most widely known truths. The probability of the fulfillment of this prophecy is 1 in 10^5.

The probability of just thirteen of the many prophecies to be fulfilled is 1 in 10^{138}. The current situation in the middle east also proves the fulfillment of several old testament prophesies. Whether you believe in the exact probability or not, the probabilities deduced for the prophecy fulfillment are still absurdly remote. The Bible record may be said to be vastly more reliable than the laws of physics. It is impossible for any serious Bible researcher to ignore the authenticity of the Scriptures.

Now let us look at John 1:1 and John 1:14.

> In the beginning was the Word, and the Word was with God, and the Word was God. (John 1:1)

> And the Word became flesh and dwelt among us, and we beheld His glory, the glory as of the only begotten of the Father, full of grace and truth. (John 1:14)

In these scriptures, God's Word is used synonymously with Jesus Christ, and we can be sure that Jesus is the Word of God personified. We also see in Revelation that Jesus Christ's name is declared to be The Word of God.

> He was clothed with a robe dipped in blood, and His name is called The Word of God. (Revelation 19:13)

We know that Jesus himself was perfect in every way. Not because He was God, but because He was a fully man. He was a person just like you and me, yet He was holy and without any sin.

> For He made Him who knew no sin to be sin for us,

that we might become the righteousness of God in Him. (2 Corinthians 5:21)

If Jesus' name is The Word of God and Jesus was perfect, we can conclude without any doubt that God's Word is indeed perfect. You will not know if this fact is actually true unless you try it for yourself by letting His Word into your heart and mind.

Also look at what Jesus says to the disciples when He appears to them after His resurrection.

> Then He said to them, "These are the words which I spoke to you while I was still with you, that all things must be fulfilled which were written in the Law of Moses and the Prophets and the Psalms concerning Me." And He opened their understanding, that they might comprehend the Scriptures. (Luke 24:44-45)

Jesus was referring to the prophecies written about Him in the Old Testament. Because Jesus is perfect, prophecies about Him in the Scriptures must be perfect. When Jesus explained the Scriptures to the disciples, why would He use imperfect Scriptures to explain His resurrection and its fulfillment? He wouldn't!

Let us look at the verse again.

> The law of the Lord is perfect, *converting* the soul. (Psalm 19:7a)

Because God's Word is perfect, it has the power to convert the soul. Herein lies the secret of human change. The soul is the inmost being that defines who a person is. It is also that which departs the human body when a person dies. It is that eternal part of the human being that lives forever. No wonder the perfect Word of God is the only tangible item that can touch a person's soul and enable it to enter heaven one day to see its Creator.

In this scripture we see that God's Word has the power to change the soul. You may be looking to many resources and remedies for the change that you want in your own life or in the life of your spouse or children. The secret to that change is God's Word. Not just reading it, for that only increases knowledge. It is the diligent study, meditation and practical implementation that converts the soul. Not only does the Word of God covert the soul, it also transforms the person into the image of God.

Here is the relationship between this characteristic and your study of God's Word.

JOSHUA 1:8	PSALM 19:7a	YOU LEARN
DO	PERFECT	APPLICATION

We commit to DO the Word because it is PERFECT to convert (transform) us through personal APPLICATION of its principles.

The Word of God is perfect, and it brings new life to one's soul.

CHAPTER 6

PERSONAL

NOTES

CHAPTER 7

GOD'S WORD

IS

SURE

In this chapter let us examine the second characteristic of God's Word that David the Psalmist documented for us.

> The testimony of the Lord is *sure*, making wise the simple. (Psalm 19:7b)

Whenever Jesus spoke, He spoke with authority. His authority came from the fact that He knew what He was saying is completely trustworthy, because His teaching came from the one who sent Him.

> And the Jews marveled, saying, "How does this Man know letters, having never studied?" Jesus answered them and said, "My doctrine is not Mine, but His who sent Me." (John 7:15-16)

Have you ever been in an argument where you had the real facts and the other person did not? You were so sure of what you were saying that you would put your life on the line, if needed. That was how sure Jesus was about His teaching. He did put His own life on the line. His sacrifice on the cross proves the trustworthiness of His teachings.

The conversion of Saul to Paul and His amazing ministry to the Jews is proof of the surety of God's Word. It has answers for every aspect of your life. It works when you implement God's direction and wisdom in your daily life. It always gives you an honest assessment of your spiritual life with no sugar coating to make it look nice. It is the only dependable advice book I have known to be trustworthy. It has proved correct every time I have applied it to my life. It gives hope when everything else seems hopeless and gives life to a dying person. It is dependable and trustworthy because it is alive.

> For the word of God is living and powerful, and sharper than any two-edged sword, piercing even to the division of soul and spirit, and of joints and marrow, and is a discerner of the thoughts and intents of the heart. (Hebrews 4:12)

Hebrews 4:12 states that the Word of God is alive. A dead person does not do anything and has no power to act or perform any activity that requires life. Because of its life, the Word of God has the power to act, to cause a change, to influence or perform actions befitting a living person.

Not only is it alive, it is also powerful. As I stated earlier, the Bible is the spoken Word of God. In Mark 4, Jesus and his disciples go out in a boat in the evening. Jesus is sleeping when a strong wind breaks out and tosses the boat. The disciples think they will drown if Jesus does not do something. I am not surprised at that thought because many times when I face difficult situations, I am looking for God to do something to save me from trouble. For the disciples, having Jesus in the boat is not enough. Eventually Jesus rebukes the wind and brings calm to the sea. The disciples are astonished.

And they feared exceedingly, and said to one another, "Who can this be, that even the wind and the sea obey Him!" (Mark 4:41)

Such is the power of Jesus' spoken Word. We also see in Luke 7 the centurion, whose servant is sick, requesting Jesus to just say the word. Jesus is amazed at the centurion's faith and His Word heals the servant.

It is important we believe that this spoken word of God written in the Scriptures is powerful to effect change in a human being.

Because the Word is living and powerful, it is like a double-edged sword that God uses to perform spiritual surgery in a willing Christian. Let me illustrate this. When someone is sick, very sick, he or she goes to the doctor who says that surgery is required. Any surgery is painful and the patient must agree to be operated upon by the doctor. So is a Christian's spiritual walk with the Lord. Every person is so depraved due to the condition of his or heart that spiritual surgery is required. The doctor is none other than our Creator. Although painful, we as believers must agree to undergo this spiritual surgery.

The surgical tool that God uses is the Word of God that is as powerful as a double edged sword (Hebrews 4:12). It can pierce through the toughest of the spiritual hearts to the inner-most being and skin out the defiled portions of the heart. You see, our hearts can be camouflaged with pre-conceived notions, a seared conscience, feelings, and emotions that create a façade to deceive us. We think that life is okay and even though the heart is very sick, a sugar-coated outward appearance provides the comfortable look that makes a Christian believe that his or her walk is adequate. Unless the double-edged sword, which is the Word of God, strikes the depravity of the heart, it cannot be fixed. God's Word is the most trusted standard that does not change with time or age or culture. It has the power to judge every human being equally and fairly.

The trustworthiness of God's Word is the key to opening our minds to the wisdom every born again Christian needs. Wisdom is the right application of the knowledge one has. It enables the believer to determine the right course of action. Just because a believer knows the Word does not make him holy. It is wisdom, the careful application of the knowledge in one's practical life that makes a Christian unique in his or her relationship with Jesus Christ.

Proverbs 3 describes the importance of gaining wisdom. God wants to give us wisdom, but that requires spiritual surgery with the Word of God. But once we get used to that surgery, it is in fact something a believer even desires so he or she can become wiser.

> She [wisdom] is more precious than rubies, And all the things you may desire cannot compare with her. (Proverbs 3:15)

In the entire Bible, there are only three books that mention the phrase, "tree of life." The first occurrence is in Genesis when God created Adam and Eve in the Garden of Eden. The garden had the tree of life along with the tree of the knowledge of good and evil (Genesis 2:9). The last occurrence is in Revelation where the tree of life is present in the Paradise of God. In Revelation 22, the river of life flowing from the throne of God had the tree of life on either side. The only other occurrence is in Proverbs, the book of wisdom. In Proverbs 3, wisdom is said to be the tree of life.

> She is a tree of life to those who take hold of her,
> And happy are all who retain her. (Proverbs 3:18)

Not only does wisdom represent the tree of life, but also those who retain her are happy or blessed. Believers gain this type of wisdom from the Word of God, which is trustworthy and sure.

Did you know that the Bible has been a best seller since its first printing? It continues to be a best seller. I use it every day to be the man that God wants me to be and to be the husband that God wants me to be. I use it to be the father that God wants me to be and to be the leader that God wants me to be. I used it to find my wife. I used it to find my job. I used it to find my calling in God's ministry. I use it when counseling someone. I use it when sharing the gospel with someone. I use it to find practical solutions to everyday problems. I have seen its power and the change it can bring about in a person's life – not only mine but in many others who believe in the surety of God's Word. When the devil tempted Jesus Christ, Jesus used God's Word because it was sure to help Him overcome Satan's temptations. In my life I have found that the Word of God is fully trustworthy. It is free, and it comes with a life-time guarantee.

What do you think about the Word of God? Is it just a fictional book or is it a factual book? Is it trustworthy enough for you to bet your life on its principles?

The Word of God is sure and it gives wisdom to the simple

who reach out to it. The renewing of your mind that is commanded in Romans 12:2 can only be achieved by the sure Word of God. If you are an avid reader of Proverbs, you will realize that this single book itself has over a hundred references to "wise" and "wisdom." Spiritual wisdom is achieved by the careful study of the Scriptures and its practical application in a believer's life.

Here is the relationship between this characteristic and your study of God's Word.

JOSHUA 1:8	PSALM 19:7b	YOU LEARN
MEDITATE	SURE	WHY/HOW

We commit to MEDITATE on the Word because it is SURE to give us wisdom. This wisdom convinces us WHY and HOW God's Word works on our minds.

The Word of God is sure, transforming the mind to comply with God's set of standards.

CHAPTER 7

PERSONAL

NOTES

CHAPTER 8

GOD'S WORD

IS

RIGHT

In this chapter let us examine the third characteristic of God's Word that David the Psalmist documented for us.

> The statutes of the LORD are *right*, rejoicing the heart. (Psalm 19:8a)

About the time I was writing this chapter, I was in a heated debate with a young lady, who was 20 at the time. We were discussing the subject of marriage and the doctrine that God has given us regarding the roles of husband and wife. Her statement several times was "but it does not make sense." And because it does not make sense, she concluded that what the Bible says must be interpreted to make sense in the current culture.

We, as Christians, must draw the line here. Just because we do not understand portions or even most of the Bible in its complete detail, does not mean that the Bible is not applicable to this age. Consider the following verse.

> For I testify to everyone who hears the words of the prophecy of this book: If anyone adds to these things, God will add to him the plagues that are written in this book; and if anyone takes away from the words of the book of this prophecy, God shall take away his

part from the Book of Life, from the holy city, and from the things which are written in this book. (Revelation 22:18-19)

Some biblical scholars consider that this verse applies not just to the book of Revelation, but to the whole New Testament and perhaps the entire Bible to ensure its contents and its canon are preserved forever and ever. So we must be careful and handle the Word of God with great care. We must not interpret it to make sense or be applicable to the current or future generations.

Consider what Jesus Christ commanded.

"You have heard that it was said, 'An eye for an eye and a tooth for a tooth.' But I tell you not to resist an evil person. But whoever slaps you on your right cheek, turn the other to him also. If anyone wants to sue you and take away your tunic, let him have your cloak also. (Matthew 5:38-40)

Does it make sense to not defend yourself when your enemy attacks you? Does it make sense that you not defend yourself in court when you are being accused? Consider still another scripture.

But brother goes to law against brother, and that before unbelievers! Now therefore, it is already an utter failure for you that you go to law against one another. Why do you not rather accept wrong? Why do you not rather let yourselves be cheated? No, you yourselves do wrong and cheat, and you do these things to your brethren! (1 Corinthians 6:6-8)

About a year ago, I was counseling a young married couple who were having problems. To protect identities, I will call them Burt and Linda. Linda had already filed for a divorce but was open to counseling to see if the marriage could be salvaged. During the course of counseling, it became apparent that both of them had to work on their relationships with God first. Both had to focus on God to heal their spiritual relationship. In addition, they both had to sever certain friendships that were hurting their marriage, which neither wanted to give up at that moment. Convinced that nothing would change, Linda eventually proceeded with the divorce. This is a classic example of a born-again couple turning away from God's direction even as they were in spiritual counseling. It did not make sense to Linda to continue to stay in the marriage. There was no doubt in her mind that divorce was the only available option. There was no sense of guilt that what she did was completely against God's commands. Linda took the route that made sense to her although it was contrary to the Word of God.

Dear Saint, the church today is becoming a huge stumbling block for the world which is looking for evidence of heaven here on earth. As more and more Christians turn away from the Bible and change it to fit their sensibilities and the next-gen culture, the need for a Savior is vanishing. Why would the world want to follow a leader that does not have true followers?

We must return to the basic foundation that every word written in the Bible is truth. It is correct in its principle and guides those who believe in Jesus Christ.

Many of you know the block buster movie *Ben-Hur: A Tale of*

Christ. The 1880 novel itself has never been out of print and outsold all books except the Bible until *Gone with the Wind* came out in 1936. But it came back to the top again in the 1960s. The film won 11 Oscars and has been seen by over a millions of people in the United States. *Ben-Hur* is also the first and only Hollywood movie ever to make it to the Vatican's official list of approved religious films. It is regularly broadcast on TV every Easter. The author of the book, General Lew Wallace has a very interesting story to tell about how the book came about. It happened on a train ride in 1875 when he met the well-known agnostic Colonel Robert Ingersoll. During this interaction on the train, Colonel Ingersoll questioned General Wallace about his faith in God, Jesus Christ as the Savior, heaven, evidence of God and many other theological aspects of the Christian faith. General Wallace did not have the answers and was ashamed of his ignorance on the subject. Challenged about his religion, he realized that he needed answers. This required the study of the Bible, any and all references he could find, and visits to multiple libraries across the nation. After seven years of research and writing, *Ben-Hur* became a reality along with a conviction in his heart to accept Jesus Christ as his personal Savior. When President Garfield finished reading *Ben-Hur*, he sent Lew Wallace a thank you note and in the same month made him the ambassador to Turkey. Ulysses S. Grant was so obsessed with the book that he confessed reading it straight for 30 hours. Many people wrote to Lew Wallace praising him for his book. Some said that it saved their lives, some said that it changed their lives, some went on to become missionaries and some even said they met Ben-Hur face to face as they read the book. The point of this reference to General Lew Wallace is that when one sincerely wants to know the truth, the Bible will become the truth for them.

In the mathematical world, one can use the Peano Postulates to prove that 1+1=2, but when we start studying in first grade, we just accept the fact that 1+1=2. We do not question the math behind it but just believe it. Today, even if a math genius has proof that 1+1 is not really 2, no one will accept it nor will it change our existing numbering system. The fact that 1+1=2 from day one in school holds true today also, even though times have changed.

We must learn to look at the Bible the same way. What God has written for us 2000 years ago and people trusted it and lived it and preached it, is still good for us today even in these changing times. We must come to the point in our lives that even if the world with its ever expanding knowledge brings proof that the Bible is not really inerrant and infallible, we should never fall into its trap. But many people seem to be so gullible and believe that portions of the Bible are not applicable to today's world. David writes this about the Word of God.

> Therefore all Your precepts concerning all things I consider to be right; I hate every false way. (Psalm 119:128)

I want to emphasize the word *consider* in this verse. David does not say that he understands everything, just that he accepts it as right, no questions asked.

We began our life with Jesus, entering into a relationship with a person that we have never met, just accepting by faith that He died for us on the cross for our sins. Having tasted and seen that the Lord is good, should we not continue in the same faith and accept every Word of God as right and every misunderstanding about it as wrong? We must, with faith, seek the counsel of the Holy Spirit when we want to understand the principles provided to us in the Bible. My attitude when I approach the Holy Spirit is that I consider and accept the Bible as right, but I do not comprehend the full practical implementation. With that attitude I am not questioning the validity of the Scriptures, but seeking to better understand them. This is how we rightly divide the word of truth.

> Be diligent to present yourself approved to God, a worker who does not need to be ashamed, rightly dividing the word of truth. (2 Timothy 2:14)

To rightly divide the word of truth we must be diligent in our study of it and careful in how we approach it. Then we will have answers to questions that the world throws at us. General Wallace could not provide the right answers to Colonel Ingersoll because he himself was not sure about God. But his study of the Scriptures and related material showed him that God does exist. Are you ready with answers when people challenge you with baffling questions? To be ready, you must accept that the Word of God is right, and is applicable to every area of a believer's life.

When one believes that the God's Word is true and trustworthy, then one begins to enjoy the freedom that it gives. Decisions are not based on questionable concepts but on proven principles. There is so much joy in knowing that what you believe is actually true and came from the one and only Almighty God.

Because the Word of God is right, it gives one the foundation to stand by it, no matter how tough the going is. When a believer follows the Bible because it is right, he or she will face persecution. Nevertheless, the believer does not give up, but will continue to trust the Word of God and will gladly endure the persecution.

Remember Richard Wurmbrand, who was famous for being tortured for Christ? Why would one endure such torture for 25 years during his second imprisonment? It has been said he maintained his sanity through exercise of his mind and soul by composing and then delivering a sermon a night. During part of his imprisonment, he communicated with other inmates by tapping Morse code messages, continuing to be a God's light to fellow inmates. Richard believed that the Word of God is right, and it brought joy to his heart no matter how inconceivably hopeless his situation was.

When we follow the Bible because it is right and we are persecuted, we are never alone.

> But we have this treasure in earthen vessels, that the excellence of the power may be of God and not of us. We are hard-pressed on every side, yet not crushed; we are perplexed, but not in despair; persecuted, but not forsaken; struck down, but not destroyed — always carrying about in the body the dying of the Lord Jesus, that the life of Jesus also may be manifested in our body. For we who live are always delivered to death for Jesus' sake, that the life of Jesus also may be manifested in our mortal flesh. (2 Corinthians 4:7-11)

The Bible promises persecution to everyone that follows the Word of God, and it reminds us not to be surprised. It advises us to count it as joy.

> My brethren, count it all joy when you fall into various trials, knowing that the testing of your faith produces patience. (James 1:2-3)

How can persecution produce joy, unless one believes that what they endure is because of something that is so right they are willing to die for it?

I remember this saying from my Sunday school teacher when I was still a very young, church-going unbeliever: "Happiness is because of good things happening to you, but real joy is because of Jesus in your heart."

Here is the relationship between this characteristic and your study of God's Word.

JOSHUA 1:8	PSALM 19:8a	YOU LEARN
DO	RIGHT	APPLICATION

We commit to DO the Word because it is just RIGHT for personal APPLICATION in our lives. When we see the results of the application, our hearts will be filled with joy that comes from Jesus.

The Word of God is indeed right, giving joy to the heart.

CHAPTER 8

PERSONAL

NOTES

CHAPTER 9

GOD'S WORD

IS

PURE

In this chapter let us examine the fourth characteristic of God's Word that David the Psalmist documented for us.

> The commandment of the LORD is *pure*, enlightening the eyes. (Psalm 19:8b)

My wife, who likes jewelry (and whose wife does not?) will not wear anything other than 24 carat gold. I remember one Valentine's Day, I bought her a very expensive diamond ring, but it was made of white gold. She would not even try it on and made me return it. Unadulterated gold, in its purest form, is a very valuable asset. The Word of God is much more than pure gold.

> More to be desired are they than gold, Yea, than much fine gold. (Psalm 19:10a)

You stand in front of a mirror to see a true reflection of yourself and make sure nothing is out of place. We do this every day, habitually. In the same way, the Bible is like the cleanest or purest of mirrors. I might dare say that even the holiest of the living saints today can stand before the biblical mirror and find some blemish in their lives that God wants to clean.

But be doers of the word, and not hearers only, deceiving yourselves. For if anyone is a hearer of the word and not a doer, he is like a man observing his natural face in a mirror; for he observes himself, goes away, and immediately forgets what kind of man he was. But he who looks into the perfect law of liberty and continues in it, and is not a forgetful hearer but a doer of the work, this one will be blessed in what he does. (James 1:22-25)

So what does this mean? For us born-again believers, it should mean that the Bible we have today is in its purest and unadulterated form as can ever be. It has the power to show us our true self: no makeup, no coverings, nothing to hide. When one stands in front the biblical mirror, the Word of God will show us who we really are.

The bigger question these days seem to be the content of the Bible. Is it really pure? How can man-written passages be considered as infallible when man himself is prone to error? Were the inclusions correct? Were the omissions correct? What if there were other texts that should have been included but were not because of human error?

This question is where our trust in the powerful Almighty comes in. One of the names of God is Elohim, which means the all-powerful God. I once did a study on this name of God, and it showed me how immense and powerful our God is. Elohim implies that God is omnipotent (all powerful), omniscient (all knowing) and omnipresent (all present). This means that our God can accomplish what He wants, however He wants, by whomever He wants, whenever He wants and wherever He wants.

It is not that hard to believe that throughout the process of developing the Bible, God was orchestrating it. He moved whoever was involved, at whatever time they were working on it, wherever they were, in a powerful and mysterious way to accomplish what He wished. But what about the canon which was used to decide which books were to be included or not? Do you not think that God could have influenced the same people deciding on the canon to do exactly what He wanted them to do? Consider,

> The king's heart is in the hand of the LORD, Like the rivers of water; He turns it wherever He wishes.
> (Proverbs 21:1)

Our God, who created the heavens and the earth with the Word of His mouth does indeed have supernatural power. He directed the hearts of everyone involved in the preparation of the Bible to accomplish exactly what He wants.

But one may question the validity of every translation that comes out and indeed that question is valid. As we are in the last days, we need to be careful about false teachers who distort the truth.

> But there were also false prophets among the people, even as there will be false teachers among you, who will secretly bring in destructive heresies, *even denying the Lord* who bought them, and bring on themselves swift destruction.
> (2 Peter 2:1)

These false teachers will make up wild theories and with impressive spiritual terminology lead many believers into false doctrine. The key principle that distinguishes them is the "even denying the Lord." We need to realize that this denial of the Lord will not be clear or outright but will be very subtle. It will be in the form of watered down gospel or compromising teachings that will appeal to many believers. These teachings have a form of spirituality that does not result in transformed lives.

I have told my church congregation many times as I stood before them that if I frequently do not step on their toes with the Word of God, it is time they started looking for a different church. Any teaching that is based on the Word of God should frequently challenge the church of God to holiness. The only mirror that should be used to show any ungodliness is the Word of God. God called us to be holy and that should be our daily desire and passion.

> Just as He chose us in Him before the foundation of the world, that we should be holy and without blame before Him in love. (Ephesians 1:4)

Any church that has no desire for holiness does not fit the "Christ and church" relationship that the Bible teaches.

> Husbands, love your wives, just as Christ also loved the church and gave Himself for her, that He might sanctify and cleanse her with the washing of water by the word, that He might present her to Himself a glorious church, not having spot or wrinkle or any such thing, but that she should be holy and without blemish. (Ephesians 5:25-27)

In this scripture, Christ loved the church and gave His life so that the church might be sanctified. Christ wants a glorious church without spot or wrinkle, so it is holy and blameless. What is it that Christ will use to cleanse the church and wash it clean? It is none other than the Word of God.

How do we know what the true Word of God is? That is where the Holy Spirit comes in. God, through His Spirit, inspired His people to write and put the Bible together. So naturally, the Spirit would be the right person to tell you what to trust. Let Him be your guide to test whatever Bible or teaching is right and compliant with the doctrinal constraints He has set up. There is the canon, or the spiritual convictions you have, or the statement of faith of the church you go to. Whatever you use, let the Spirit guide you regarding its compliance with the strictest of doctrinal principles of the true Word of God.

The Word of God becomes the ultimate standard. But the standard itself was set by God through the Holy Spirit. He inspired common people to pull together the Bible that withstands the test of time, culture, generations, and changes that we have seen and will see.

The Word of God is pure and that is the most important reason that we should look into it as a mirror to check our spiritual life. When we do that, we get the purest assessment of our spiritual life. It will show us how much has changed since we became a born-again Christian and what else needs to change before our Lord returns. This is where we experience enlightenment as the Word brings mystery into practical realm. That is exactly what Psalm 19:8 means. This is the enlightenment that the entire world is looking for everywhere else, except in the Word of God. We must be careful we do not fall prey to worldly enlightenment, but rather rely on the Scriptures, a pure mirror, to enlighten our eyes that we might see.

Only the pure Word of God can enlighten our eyes that we may see our spiritual growth.

Here is the relationship between this characteristic and your study of God's Word.

JOSHUA 1:8	PSALM 19:8b	YOU LEARN
READ	PURE	WHAT

We commit to READ the Word because it is PURE telling us WHAT God requires of us. It opens our eyes to the powerful standard we are called to live by. May we depend on nothing else but the pure Word of God.

In this and the previous three chapters, we looked at four characteristics of the Word of God.

The Word of God is perfect and has the power to bring a sinner to repentance. It has the power to enable a born-again believer to walk in holiness and turn from sin to God. It works on the soul.

The Word of God is sure, giving wisdom as it transforms the mind, which is a complex entity. Only something that is proven accurate can penetrate the logical nature of the brain. It works on the mind.

The Word of God is right providing the balance that a Christian needs to live a holy life in this unholy world. When things don't seem right, the Word of God provides us the confidence and the right perspective. It ensures that joy will override any discomfort of the heart. It works on the heart.

The Word of God is pure, giving us the wisdom. It provides the enlightenment we need to have a higher perspective of what God is doing in us to transform us into a holy and blameless church. It works on our strength.

> And you shall love the LORD your God with all your heart, with all your soul, with all your mind, and with all your strength. (Mark 12:30)

You see, it is impossible to keep the first commandment that Jesus gave us without clearly understanding the four characteristics of the Word of God and the power it has over our soul, heart, mind and strength.

I urge you to make a commitment to diligently study the Word of God. Let it be your standard for every day choices. Only then will your life be *Word Driven*.

CHAPTER 9

PERSONAL

NOTES

CHAPTER 10

WORD DRIVEN

To be *Word driven*, a believer must become a serious disciple of the Word of God. Christians complain that God does not reveal Himself to them. God does want to reveal himself to us, but He does that through His Word.

Christians will not take the time to read the Word, but want God to reveal Himself through visions, or voices or a strong feeling. But there is a danger in depending on these types of revelations as Satan himself can appear as an angel of light and lead people astray. The Bible is the most trusted and infallible method of God revealing Himself to us through His Son Jesus Christ.

During my counseling sessions, people will say that "God told me" to do this. My immediate response is always, "How did God tell you?" Their response will be, "It is one of my spiritual gifts or God laid a burden on my heart or I have this strong feeling."

That, my dear saints, is a very dangerous method of finding God's direction. There is risk associated with it, and Christians take that risk without understanding the consequences of their actions. They strongly believe they are following God's direction without recognizing the danger. They think nothing can go wrong, and when things do go wrong, they blame God for it. Being *Word Driven* is summarized in Joshua 1:8. Let us review that scripture again.

This Book of the Law shall not depart from your

mouth, but you shall meditate in it day and night, that you may observe to do according to all that is written in it. For then you will make your way prosperous, and then you will have good success. (Joshua 1:8)

According to Joshua 1:8, you and I have to do three things with respect to God's Word. First, we are to READ the Word. We commit to READ the Word because it gives us PURE enlightenment so we know WHAT we are required to do.

Next, we are to MEDITATE on the Word. We commit to MEDITATE on the Word because it gives us SURE wisdom so we know WHY and HOW we comply with God's direction.

Finally we are to DO WHAT God's Word tells us to do. We commit to DO what God directs us to do because through APPLICATION we see that God's direction is PERFECT and just RIGHT for us.

To put it simply, being *Word Driven* is READ THE BIBLE, THINK THE BIBLE, and DO THE BIBLE. Memorize this caption – Read it, think it, do it! But this reading, thinking and applying the Bible must be done in a disciplined way. Then it shows God you do regard this activity with Jesus the most important part of each day.

Here is a step by step approach to improve your consistency of spending time with the Word every day. This is referred to as Quiet Time (QT)

a.) Setup a time each day that you will meet Jesus Christ, whether it is in the morning or in the evening depending on your work schedule. For me, since I work a normal 7-5 schedule, I make it a point to have my QT before I go to work. My mind is fresh in the morning after a good night's rest and is receptive of what God wants to teach me for that day. Scriptures tell us that Jesus went off to a solitary place very early in the morning to pray. So find a quiet place first thing in the morning to have your quiet time. If you have never done this before, I recommend starting with one day a week and disciplining yourself. A few weeks later, add another day and work towards having your QT every day. Typically one can accomplish this practice within a few months, but don't worry if it takes a little longer.

b.) Re-arrange your daily schedule to make this appointment with God. You go to work on time, keep your professional appointments on time, and take your kids to school on time. Should you not keep your appointment with God and be there on time? This is one way you show God that He is the first priority in your life.

c.) If you have never had a habit of having your QT every day, begin with the gospel of John. Do not read a whole chapter or multiple chapters at a time. Most Bibles have sections with titles within each chapter. Read one section only. Read it again if you have trouble grasping the content. Ask God to speak to you and don't rush your time with the Lord.

d.) If you come across a principle, take some time to meditate on it. It could be a command to follow, a sin to confess, a promise to hold on to or just simple advice. Memorize the scripture and through the day meditate on it. As you face situations or choices throughout the day, think about how that particular principle can be applied.

e.) At the end of the day, before you go to bed, examine your day. Assess your handling of the day, or the choices you made, or your responses to situations. Were they consistent with the Word that you read? If not what could you have done better?

f.) As you get better at your QT, add a chapter of proverbs to your reading for the day. Read Proverbs 1:1-7 and you will quickly realize how important the book of Proverbs can be for our daily life. How many chapters there are in Proverbs? How many days are there in a month? I don't believe that is a coincidence. One chapter for every day of the month! I believe God has given us an opportunity to read a chapter of proverbs each day of the month. If you miss reading proverbs that day, do not worry. Just go on to the next day. Proverbs is a host of spiritual principles that I have used each day of my life.

For first time practitioners of QT, the principle here is to form a habit of having your QT every day. As you meet God face to face each day, you will not only enjoy your time with God but begin to see God work in your everyday life.

The next method is a little bit more difficult and for some Christians, it may look like it is an impossible task. Nevertheless, you must work hard at it as this is what helped Jesus when he faced Satan. He used the Word of God that he had memorized. I am referring to scripture memory. Chuck Swindoll wrote, "I know of no other single practice in the

Christian life more rewarding, practically speaking, than memorizing scripture. No other single exercise pays greater spiritual dividends! Your prayer life will be strengthened. Your witnessing will be sharper and much more effective. Your attitudes and outlook will begin to change. Your mind will become alert and observant. Your confidence and assurance will be enhanced. Your faith will be solidified" (*Growing Strong in the Seasons of Life* [Grand Rapids: Zondervan, 1994], p. 61).

I agree. Scripture memory has revolutionized my personal walk with the Lord. Apart from overcoming Satan, there are other benefits we receive by memorizing scripture. Some of them are –

a.) We learn how to conform ourselves to Christ's image, the same image in which God created Adam and Eve.

The fear of the Lord is the beginning of wisdom and knowledge of the Holy One is understanding. (Proverbs 9:10)

Knowing God's character is primary for us to imitate Him. How can we imitate Him unless we know who He is?

b.) We know how to counsel those in need of prayer and comfort.

A word fitly spoken is like apples of gold in settings of silver. (Proverbs 25:11)

I picked up a beautiful saying somewhere which says the same thing. *When a heart full of God's love can draw on the mind full of God's Word, timely blessings flow from the mouth.*

c.) We know how to pray better.

> Likewise the Spirit also helps in our weaknesses. For we do not know what we should pray for as we ought, but the Spirit Himself makes intercession for us with groanings which cannot be uttered. (Romans 8:26)

The Spirit uses the scriptures that we have memorized and richly enhances our communion with God Almighty.

d.) We know how to share God's gospel of peace.

> Preach the word! Be ready in season and out of season. Convince, rebuke, exhort, with all longsuffering and teaching. (2 Timothy 4:2)

I had numerous occasions to share the gospel with strangers. If I did not know and memorize the scriptures, I could not have answered their questions about God's love through His son Jesus Christ. People don't want to listen to my opinion, but they will listen when you say, "The Bible says…"

Let me address how the brain stores information to help us

understand how to memorize scripture. The brain stores information as sensory memory, short term memory or long term memory. The goal in scripture memory is to move the memory of the various parts of a scripture verse to long term memory and ensure it stays active for retrieval. Experts believe that the hippocampus and the frontal cortex are the two parts of the brain that decide what is worth remembering. Repeated sensory input of the same information to the brain is believed to be the one reason that makes information worth remembering. Once the decision is made that certain information is worth remembering, it is moved into long term memory.

Hence it is common practice to repeat aloud something over and over again to memorize it. When you practice repetition, your brain is also establishing links between the various pieces of information that can be later assembled together for retrieval. When you memorize a reference, the verse and an associated topic, you are establishing links between them, just like data in a relational database. Later, when you think of a topic, the associated verse and reference automatically come up or vice versa.

But one issue that we need to take care of is the latency of the data being written. As time goes by, the brain thinks that the data has not been accessed and so it is okay to write over it or break the links and re-use the memory. To keep the data active, one must refresh the validity of the data with scripture review. When you review the verses on a periodic basis, you refresh the validity of what is already in your memory telling the brain not to overwrite it with something else.

Here is a secret that we all need to understand. The renewing of your mind stated in Romans 12:2 is accomplished by memorizing scripture verses and reviewing them regularly. You will be amazed at how this actually works. Try it and see for yourself. God has given us a brain that is complex and powerful. He wants us to use it wisely.

How do we discipline ourselves in memorizing scripture? Here is a step by step approach that you can use for this exercise. No matter what approach you use, memorize one scripture verse a week.

a.) First find a set of scriptures that have a topic associated with them. I have used the Navigator's Topical Memory System (TMS) available at www.navpress.com. Whatever you use, come up with a set of scripture memory verses. Write them as a list in your journal, if you keep one or print a list out and put it up on the fridge. If you use the TMS, this is already done for you via a set of cards printed with the reference, the topic and the verse.

b.) Select a verse for that week and during your QT, read that verse several times. Understand the gist of the verse and its importance to your spiritual walk. This associates the verse with something important in your life.

c.) Memorize the reference first. This is similar to kids getting ready for a school spelling bee. We have twin girls who were nine years old at the time of writing this book. My wife helped them get ready for the spelling bee at school. If they made a simple mistake, they repeated the spelling three times. If they made a major mistake, they repeated it five times. This helped them dramatically to remember the spellings. Do the same with the reference.

Repeat the reference over and over again, so when you begin to say it, it flows out smoothly.

d.) Next memorize the topic. If you don't remember the entire verse completely, you now have a cross reference between the topic and the reference of your verse. This will help you look up the verse if needed. These days with a complete Bible available on your smart phone, just knowing the scripture reference and the topic will help you get by. This is helpful when you have to counsel or share the gospel. Use the same approach as before and say the reference and topic several times. By doing so, you establish a link between the reference and the topic. So when you think about the topic, the reference comes up automatically, or vice versa.

e.) Next memorize the scripture verse completely verbatim. Whatever version you chose to use, you must memorize it exactly as it is written. Break up the verse into chunks of phrases and start with the reference, then the topic and then add a phrase from the verse. Once you are done with that, add another phrase and so on. Doing this establishes links between the reference, the topic and the various phrases that make up the verse. By repetition and association you move all parts of the scripture verse to your long term memory. Adding verses to your memory every week results in erasing old data and writing in new data.

f.) Go on to the next verse the following week. At the end of each week, review all the verses you have memorized so far. By reviewing the verses, you are refreshing the validity of the verses in your memory, so the brain will not erase them with other data.

g.) The next step is very important. Find an accountability partner to meet with on a regular basis. If you both are memorizing the same scriptures, then you can check on each other. You can do this in person, or over the phone, or via FaceTime or Skype. This is a good marriage builder, too, when you do this with your spouse.

As you discipline yourself in your quiet time and scripture memory, you will strengthen your personal relationship with Christ. He not only is your Savior, but will become your master and friend. He becomes your soul mate as you fall deeply in love with him.

I urge you to diligently READ the Word, MEDITATE on the Word and APPLY (DO) the Word in every aspect of your life. Only then will your life be *Word Driven.*

CHAPTER 10

PERSONAL

NOTES

CHAPTER 11

THE POWER

OF

THE HOLY SPIRIT

He hovered over the waters as God created the heavens and the earth. He empowered Gideon who choose just three hundred men and defeated the Mideanites. He descended as a dove on Jesus Christ when John baptized Him. He is the seven fold Spirit of God as described in Isaiah 11:2. Any blasphemy against Him will not be forgiven. He was there when I first accepted Jesus as my Savior, and He continues to work in my life as I make Jesus my Master.

We have looked at the Word and the power it can have in your life. Now let us see how and where the second person, The Holy Spirit, fits into the transformation process. We will see how the Holy Spirit comes *alongside* to convict the sinner, and then *indwells* in the born-again believer and finally *fills* the believer. This is the three phased process involving the Holy Spirit as He transforms a sinner into a living sacrifice that is holy and acceptable to God.

> I beseech you therefore, brethren, by the mercies of God, that you present your bodies a living sacrifice, holy, acceptable to God, which is your reasonable service. (Romans 12:1)

Let me illustrate the role of the Holy Spirit using an age old tradition that has been followed in India. This is the tradition of matchmaking. For a fee, a marriage broker will bring ten to fifteen pictures of beautiful prospective brides to the groom's parents for their review. The groom's parents then review the pictures and select one they believe is right for their son. At this point the work of the marriage broker is done while the parents continue the coordination of the marriage.

The relationship between Jesus Christ and the born-again Christian is described as a marriage in the Bible. Similar to a marriage broker for an earthly marriage, there is a marriage broker for the spiritual marriage that starts here on earth but continues on into heaven and into eternity. That spiritual marriage broker is the Holy Spirit himself. I call him the Celestial Marriage Broker.

To understand the role of the Holy Spirit in this spiritual marriage, we must first understand the nature of the marriage. The actual spiritual wedding does not take place until Christ returns. Revelation paints a picture of what happens at the wedding.

> And I heard, as it were, the voice of a great multitude, as the sound of many waters and as the sound of mighty thunderings, saying, "Alleluia! For the Lord God Omnipotent reigns! Let us be glad and rejoice and give Him glory, for the marriage of the Lamb has come, and His wife has made herself ready." And to her it was granted to be arrayed in fine linen, clean and bright, for the fine linen is the righteous acts of the saints. (Revelation 19:6-8)

There are few important things that we need to clearly

understand here. First, we read that the marriage of the Lamb has come. This means that today the church, being the bride of the Lamb, is still getting ready to meet the Lamb, Jesus Christ, who is the groom. Second, we see that the bride has made herself ready. During this waiting period, from the time the bride was introduced to Jesus Christ (at the point of salvation) to the time she meets Jesus face to face for the actual wedding, she has been carefully preparing herself. Third, we see that the bride was given fine linen representing the righteousness of the bride. The bride here is none other than the church.

To better understand the entire meaning of this scripture, let me give a brief description of the Jewish wedding process. The very first step in a Jewish wedding is the matchmaking process. The groom's father calls a *Shadchan,* the match-maker, to select a bride for his son. Once that selection is completed and both sets of parents agree on the match, a betrothal is then planned. The betrothal is a ceremony where a marriage covenant is established between the bride and the groom. This is similar to an engagement in today's culture, except that it cannot be broken. During the betrothal ceremony, the groom places a betrothal ring on the bride's finger. This ring signifies a seal or a reminder to the bride and everyone else that the bride is already spoken for and that the bridegroom will come back for his bride after a certain period of time. As part of the betrothal, the bridegroom negotiates the price (mohar) with the bride's father. This is the price he will pay to purchase his bride. Nullifying the betrothal is equivalent to a divorce. As a symbol of this agreement, the bride and groom drink from a cup of wine that has been blessed. The bridegroom then leaves the bride in her father's house and returns to his father's house where he proceeds to prepare a place for his bride. During this time, the bride carefully prepares herself, waiting for the expected return of her husband to take her back to his father's house and consummate the marriage. Interestingly, it is the groom's father who determines when his son is ready to go bring his bride to live with them.

You might already have seen the similarities between the Jewish wedding and the spiritual wedding between the church and our Lord Jesus Christ. Let me focus on the spiritual *Shadchan*, the Celestial Marriage Broker. He brokers the marriage covenant between the individuals that make up the church and the Lord Jesus Christ. He does this based on His intimate knowledge of both parties involved.

Let us start with the first introduction between the sinner and the savior. Have you ever heard your friend or someone say "He got saved because of me?" We need to be very careful about such statements as we are taking credit for something we did not do. No human being has the power to convert a person or make a person believe in Jesus Christ. When we share the gospel, we bear witness to what Christ has done in our own lives. The actual conviction is accomplished by the Holy Spirit. He, because of his intimate knowledge of the condition of the sinner's heart and the unconditional love of Jesus Christ, has the power to convict a sinner of his or her need for the Savior.

> And when He has come, He will convict the world of sin, and of righteousness, and of judgment: of sin, because they do not believe in Me. (John 16:8-9)

> Therefore I make known to you that no one speaking by the Spirit of God calls Jesus accursed, and no one can say that Jesus is Lord except by the Holy Spirit. (1 Corinthians 12:3)

The Holy Spirit comes *alongside* the sinner and introduces the sinner to the Savior. But you may say that you don't see or feel his presence at salvation. A good way to explain that is using the concept of floodlighting a building or monument or an architectural structure. When an engineer looks to lighting up a building, there are two requirements. One is that the building's form, beauty and architectural identify is not disturbed or obscured. The second is that the building should be illuminated to a level that reveals its texture and the character of the architectural design. The trick to doing this is to hide the floodlights so that they are not seen nor do they obscure the view of the building. That is how the Holy Spirit works. He is right there, but the focus is not on him, the marriage broker, but on the groom, Jesus Christ. He never says, "Look at me, I am the one who made this happen." Rather, He says, "Look at Jesus, your groom, your future husband; trust in Him; love him." The Holy Spirit is the hidden floodlight illuminating Jesus Christ and His character so we may see every detail of His beauty and His love, and fall in love with Him. This is the first task of the celestial marriage broker – coming alongside to introduce the sinner to the savior.

When a person meets Jesus Christ for the first time, unknown to us, a betrothal celebration takes place. At this time of salvation, as the person (the bride) is betrothed to Jesus Christ (the groom), the angels in heaven are celebrating this betrothal.

> Likewise, I say to you, there is joy in the presence of the angels of God over one sinner who repents. (Luke 15:10)

While the angels are celebrating, the groom, Jesus Christ, is confirming His commitment to the bride by placing a *ring* as a sign or seal of His return. This seal is the Holy Spirit.

> In Him you also trusted, after you heard the word of truth, the gospel of your salvation; in whom also, having believed, you were sealed with the Holy Spirit of promise, who is the guarantee of our inheritance until the redemption of the purchased possession, to the praise of His glory. (Ephesians 1:13-14)

Unlike the marriage brokers of the world whose job is done with the betrothal, this celestial marriage broker, the Holy Spirit, continues to stay with the bride to help her prepare for the groom's return.

> However, when He, the Spirit of truth, has come, He will guide you into all truth; for He will not speak on His own authority, but whatever He hears He will speak; and He will tell you things to come. He will glorify Me, for He will take of what is Mine and declare it to you. (John 16:13-14)

Let us examine the above scripture. There are four subjects in it. The main subject is obviously the Holy Spirit referred to as "He" nine times. Then there is "you," meaning every born-again Christian that makes up the bride of Christ. Next there is "Me," referring to Jesus Christ himself, and finally there is the Father. Herein are all the ingredients required to prepare the bride for Christ's return. Not only is the Holy Spirit the marriage broker, He now transitions to be a permanent marriage counselor who continues to illuminate Jesus Christ and teaches the bride (you and me) everything we need to learn about our future husband, Jesus Christ. He does this now by *indwelling* in us as the seal of Jesus' commitment to come back for us.

> Do you not know that you are the temple of God and that the Spirit of God dwells in you? (1 Corinthians 3:16)

> But the Helper [counselor, NIV], the Holy Spirit, whom the Father will send in My name, He will teach you all things, and bring to your remembrance all things that I said to you. (John 14:26)

The above scripture is significant for us as we learn to understand how the Holy Spirit affects the transformation in our lives. He does this from the inside out, not from the outside in. From a human standpoint, change is normally affected by controlling the behavior, which is from the outside. From a spiritual standpoint, change has to be affected by changing the heart, which is from the inside. All through the preparation period, from the time a sinner is born-again to the time Christ returns, the Holy Spirit is slowly working on the condition of the heart.

When I first met Jesus Christ, I wanted to please him so much. I tried to stop doing what I knew was wrong and tried to do what I knew was right. But I had the same dilemma as Paul.

> For what I am doing, I do not understand. For what I

will to do, that I do not practice; but what I hate, that I do. (Romans 7:15)

This dilemma can only be overcome when the Holy Spirit *fills* the believer. It wasn't until I figured out what it meant to be filled with the Holy Spirit, that I started seeing changes in my heart. We will study this concept in Chapter 16.

If we allow him to, He, the marriage counselor, will teach us, train us, clean house (the heart) and prepare us for Christ's return.

The Holy Spirit, the celestial marriage broker, came *alongside* and introduced us to Jesus Christ. When we accepted Jesus Christ as our savior, He began to *indwell* in us and became our permanent life counselor. Now let Him *fill* us with His power and teach us to get ready for the beautiful wedding waiting for us. We must not only learn to recognize the presence and counsel of the Holy Spirit, but also learn to submit to His direction.

To be led by the Holy Spirit we must understand the Holy Spirit power required for this incredible and supernatural transformation from a sinful life to a holy life. But this transformation is not perfected overnight. Rather, it is a progressive holiness realized over time as the believer prepares his or her heart for the spiritual wedding to come.

In the next few chapters we will examine the seven-fold Spirit of God as described in Isaiah 11:2. We will understand how He works this amazing transformation as we are *Spirit Led.*

CHAPTER 11

PERSONAL

NOTES

CHAPTER 12

THE SPIRIT

OF

THE LORD

Let us understand the nature of the Holy Spirit by examining Isaiah 11:2.

> The Spirit of the LORD shall rest upon Him,
> The Spirit of wisdom and understanding,
> The Spirit of counsel and might,
> The Spirit of knowledge and of the fear of the
> LORD. (Isaiah 11:2)

Notice that the Holy Spirit described above was to rest on Jesus Christ in this prophetic statement of His coming. This same Spirit with these seven characteristics was to fill Him and empower Him to carry out the sole purpose of His coming to this world. Seven, in the Bible, signifies completeness. Hence, this seven-fold Spirit of God, possessing every aspect of the transforming power, can give us everything required to complete the work God has started in every born-again believer. A believer must believe that the Holy Spirit indwelling within comes with fullness, completeness and perfection and does not require any more of the Holy Spirit than what is already indwelling within the believer.

Mary conceived Jesus Christ by the power of the Holy Spirit.

Jesus Christ started His official ministry only after He was baptized by John and the Spirit of God descended upon Him like a dove. After He was baptized, the Spirit took Him into the wilderness to be tempted by the devil. Jesus was filled with the Holy Spirit when He defeated Satan and his temptations. At the day of Pentecost, the disciples were filled with the Holy Spirit and spoke in tongues. It is of the same Spirit that the Scriptures say-

> But he who blasphemes against the Holy Spirit never has forgiveness, but is subject to eternal condemnation. (Mark 3:29)

Some have diminished the deity of the Holy Spirit because He is the third person of the Godhead. The Spirit is no less than God the Father and God the Son. The Spirit is God Himself. Hence He is called the Spirit of God and the Holy Spirit.

Some scholars represent the characteristics of the Holy Spirit, in conjunction with Isaiah 11:2, as the Golden Lampstand placed in the tabernacle.

In Isaiah 11:2, the seven characteristics of the Holy Spirit are stated starting with one stand-alone characteristic and the remaining six grouped in pairs of two. This is similar to the lampstand with a stand-alone center stand and three pairs of branches on either side of the center stand.

The center stand represents the Spirit of God and can stand alone without any of the other branches. It is the core, the basis, the stand, the foundation, or the pillar from whom the rest of the six supernatural characteristics branch out. The six branches are attached to the center stand meaning that they do not exist by themselves apart from the Spirit of God. This attachment symbolizes the Holy Spirit as the only source of truth regarding God and His relationship with us.

> However, when He, the Spirit of truth, has come, He will guide you into all truth; for He will not speak on His own authority, but whatever He hears He will speak; and He will tell you things to come. (John 16:13)

Many churches today are falling away from the truth because they are not looking to the Spirit of God. Apart from the Holy Spirit, pastors are teaching a compromised gospel and leading thousands away from God. Without complete and full dependence on the Holy Spirit, no pastor can teach the biblical truth to the congregation.

Continuing with the lampstand, the stand and the branches all end in a lamp. These seven lamps were to be filled with olive oil to keep the lamps burning continuously giving light to the priests working the temple. The Holy Spirit in the same way becomes the permanently burning light and never goes out. He continuously prepares the bride for the wonderful return of the bridegroom.

Notice that the entire lampstand is made of pure gold. Throughout the Bible, gold of the purest form was used to make things in the temple and to describe the holiness of God.

> For such a High Priest was fitting for us, who is holy, harmless, undefiled, separate from sinners, and has become higher than the heavens. (Hebrews 7:26)

The lampstand made of pure gold symbolizes that the Spirit is holy and undefiled. Such a Spirit can only be of God who is holy. The entire lampstand was hammered out from a single piece of gold. This symbolizes the fact that the Holy Spirit comes from God with the seven characteristics associated with Him. One cannot receive the Spirit of God and not have access to these seven characteristics. These are not the gifts that come with the Holy Spirit but are inherent abilities available to every born-again believer. And these characteristics are pure, giving the believer the brightest light needed to see the things of God clearly.

The very first of the seven-fold Spirit is the fact that the Spirit is of God or of the Lord. This is the most important characteristic of the Holy Spirit. Not only is the Spirit from God, it is the Spirit of the Lord. It is this Spirit that enabled Jesus Christ as a human being to stand firm and live a perfect holy life. Jesus started His earthly ministry right after His baptism when He received the Holy Spirit descending on Him like a dove. You might question the necessity of Jesus needing to be filled with the Holy Spirit. Remember that when Jesus gave up His throne and His crown, he made

Himself of no reputation and became like a bondservant in the likeness of a human being. Taking the form of a human being, He gave up His Godly privileges. This does not mean that he gave up being God; just that He gave up His privileges. He did this to show every believer, that, although He became a man, He set the supreme example of surrendering His life to God in obedience. Empowered by the Spirit of God, He accomplished everything to glorify God.

Now let us look at another passage that describes the Holy Spirit.

> If you love Me, keep My commandments. And I will pray the Father, and He will give you *another* Helper, that He may abide with you forever. (John 14:15-16)

Jesus challenges us here that if we really love Him, we should keep His commandments. But He also knows that it is impossible for us to meet this challenge alone. Immediately He assures us that He has a plan. This plan includes *another* Helper. This means that a helper of the same kind as Jesus will be available to us. This helper will have all the same abilities that Jesus has, including the privilege of being God, to abide with (indwell in) us forever.

The first act of being led by the Holy Spirit is the recognition that the Spirit we receive at conversion (being born-again) is of the same nature of Jesus Christ. He has all the privileges of God, being given to us with all fullness and completeness, apart from which, any resemblance of Godly transformation is impossible.

The core, The Spirit of the Lord, branches out in pairs

enabling in us several supernatural abilities. These abilities are required for the transformation that God wants in every believer. Apart from these, a Christian has no ability to imitate Jesus Christ.

Only by the Spirit of the Lord can we become living sacrifices, holy, and acceptable to God.

CHAPTER 12

PERSONAL

NOTES

CHAPTER 13

THE SPIRIT

OF

WISDOM

AND

UNDERSTANDING

As we saw in the previous chapter, the main stand in the lamp-stand has three pairs of branches. Each pair of branches symbolizes a pair of supernatural abilities that the Holy Spirit gives to us.

In this chapter, we will discuss the first pair of branches describing the wisdom and understanding of the Holy Spirit.

Many verses in Proverbs speak of wisdom and understanding. One particular verse I like is -

> Wisdom is the principle thing; Therefore get wisdom. In all your getting get understanding. (Proverbs 4:7)

The same verse in another version tells us to get wisdom even though it costs us everything we have. Solomon having "been there, done that" comes to this very important recognition that wisdom and understanding are essential for life to have any reasonable meaning. Deuteronomy 4:5,6 defines wisdom as the ability to practically apply biblical knowledge gained from the study of God's Word. In other words, wisdom is the ability to determine the difference between Godly and worldly in your quest to live a Godly life. We can learn from the incident in the Garden of Eden when Eve ate of the tree of knowledge of good and evil to gain wisdom.

> So when the woman saw that the tree was good for food, that it was pleasant to the eyes, and a tree desirable to make one wise, she took of its fruit and ate. She also gave to her husband with her, and he ate. (Genesis 3:6)

Eve somehow concluded that the very approach that God warned her about was the approach she had to take to gain wisdom. In a similar way, believers today are following Eve's example for gaining wisdom – following the very path that Jesus warned us about.

> Do not love the world or the things in the world. If anyone loves the world, the love of the Father is not in him. For all that is in the world — the lust of the flesh, the lust of the eyes, and the pride of life — is not of the Father but is of the world. And the world is passing away, and the lust of it; but he who does the will of God abides forever. (1 John 2:15-17)

Instead of heeding to this warning, churches continue to teach and follow what I call the CAN principle. They follow what is Common, Acceptable and Normal by the world's standards. Churches are increasingly finding it hard to preach the uncompromising gospel because they are afraid they will lose their congregation. Eventually these churches produce ineffective Christians stagnated in their personal growth and relationship with the Lord.

Consequentially, they become stumbling blocks to the next generation of Christians because of the sin that continues in their life. It is clear that Bible-based living is declining with each generation. The NexGen kids do not seem to have the passion or even the desire to look to the Bible for life principles.

Understanding is defined as the ability to expand the breadth and depth of God's direction in your quest to live a Godly life. Paul writes to the Philippians and explains.

> And this I pray, that your love may abound still more and more in knowledge and all discernment, that you may approve the things that are excellent, that you may be sincere and without offense till the day of Christ, being filled with the fruits of righteousness which are by Jesus Christ, to the glory and praise of God. (Philippians 1:9-11)

Quite often counselors use psychology and worldly techniques to resolve problems in life because of the lack of understanding of Godly principles. The medical field is constantly inventing new drugs to treat problems that have to do with sinful nature of man. Rather than realizing that the heart must be treated with Godly medicine, pastors and counselors are resorting to worldly methods. People want to see immediate results and when these methods see immediate improvement, although temporary, this becomes the primary method of treating spiritual sickness.

For God to transform our lives, a believer must seek wisdom and understanding from God that comes through the enabling power of the Holy Spirit. Look at what Moses tells the children of Israel.

> Surely I have taught you statutes and judgments, just
> as the LORD my God commanded me, that you
> should act according to them in the land which you
> go to possess. Therefore be careful to observe them;
> for this is your wisdom and your understanding in the
> sight of the peoples who will hear all these statutes,
> and say, 'Surely this great nation is a wise and
> understanding people.' (Deuteronomy 4:5-6)

Moses is crystal clear as he instructs Israel to observe God's
commands. The world will only recognize the uniqueness of
Jesus Christ, if our wisdom and understanding of God's
principles is evidenced in our personal life. So how does the
Holy Spirit enable us to be wise and understanding?
Supernaturally! And that is why many Christians fail to
recognize this capability in their lives. They are looking for
humanly reasonable ways to be wise and understanding. We
must stop looking and start accepting that the indwelling
Holy Spirit is capable of accomplishing this supernatural
activity in our everyday lives. In the earlier chapters we saw
how a Christian should be *Word driven*.

Reading the Word provides a renewed mind that the Holy
Spirit will reprogram with the right kind of understanding.
This enables you to understand WHAT God wants you to do
in your life.

Meditating on the Word opens up the door for the Holy
Spirit to show you how to translate your understanding of
God's principles into applicable doctrine for your life. This
enables you to understand WHY God wants you to follow

His rules and HOW to make right choices for your life.

> Through wisdom a house is built, And by
> understanding it is established. (Proverbs 24:3)

Obtaining Godly wisdom and understanding go hand in hand with being *Word driven*. Many believers want this wisdom and understanding but will not take the time to sit down and read the Bible and meditate on it. Without this diligent practice of spending time with the Word, Godly wisdom and understanding can never be gained.

If you thirst for Godly wisdom and understanding, then you must drink from the Word of God. When you sit down to have your devotions or Quiet Time with the Lord as I discussed in Chapter 10, add these simple steps.

a.) First of all, pray. Tell God that you acknowledge Him as the only source of wisdom and understanding. Pray and ask Him to enlighten you through the Holy Spirit as you read His Word.

b.) Second, read the portion of the Word designated for your devotion. As you read, talk things out with the Holy Spirit. Whether you talk aloud or just in your heart, it does not matter. As you read, try to understand the passage. Read it again if you don't get it first. The Holy Spirit works well when your mind is fertile with God's Word. Let Him filter out the worldly junk and enable you to see the purest of understanding that can come from God's Word. He does this by opening your mind and heart to a deeper and wider meaning of the passage you are reading. Every time you read the same passage you will see it in a new light. The Holy Spirit adds to your knowledge and wisdom each time you read the passage.

c.) Let me address Bible study guides here. I use them frequently to see what other biblical scholars have to say about a particular difficult passage. I only look to trusted scholars. Talk to your pastor or home group leader if a particular commentary or exposition is trustworthy. If an explanation borders on the weird or worldly, throw it away. Do not even waste a second on it. It is important that you depend on the Holy Spirit to show you what is Godly and what is worldly. He will either remind you of a verse from the Bible or a doctrinal principle that can help you decipher whether the subject matter is Godly or worldly. Do not depend on your own understanding, because your natural self will want to believe what it wants to please itself. Rather you must learn and practice every day to let the Holy Spirit lead you in this process of discerning what is Godly and what is not.

d.) After understanding the basic premise of the passage, you are ready to transition knowledge into practical application. Think about how the passage could make a difference in your life. Does it change your goals or what your life's end state should be? Does your understanding of the passage change how you go about making right choices that please God? When you think or meditate, use the following scripture to guide you.

> Finally, brethren, whatever things are true, whatever things are noble, whatever things are just, whatever things are pure, whatever things are lovely, whatever

things are of good report, if there is any virtue and if there is anything praiseworthy — meditate on these things. (Philippians 4:8)

As you meditate on the passage, the Holy Spirit points out important principles you need in your life. If the passage talks about a particular sin that you are currently engaged in, the Holy Spirit convicts you. Or perhaps you see a financial principle to help you manage your finances better. Or perhaps you see a principle that helps you develop a better relationship with your wife and children. The Holy Spirit helps by showing you from God's Word why a particular choice is right or wrong in God's sight. Many make wrong choices without knowing they are wrong. By meditating on the passage you allow the Holy Spirit to influence your thought process based on the Word of God.

e.) Keep a journal if your mind is not capable of being your journal. Make notes so that you don't forget the principles you have learned. Write down the scriptures that back up your understanding so that you are convinced that no other standard is acceptable to God other than what the Holy Spirit revealed to you. Whatever the biblical principle you learned that day, document it in your mind or your journal, so you can refer back to it as a refresher.

f.) Lastly, close in prayer. Make a commitment to God regarding the principle and the changes you are going to make in your life. Ask the Holy Spirit to guide you and empower you to follow through on your commitments.

Here is the relationship between these two enablers (understanding and wisdom) from the Holy Spirit and your study of the Word of God.

JOSHUA 1:8	ISAIAH 11:2	YOU LEARN
READ	UNDERSTANDING	WHAT
MEDITATE	WISDOM	WHY/HOW

When you READ the Word of God, the Holy Spirit will give you the UNDERSTANDING to learn WHAT GOD wants for your life. When you MEDITATE on the Word of God, the Holy Spirit will give the WISDOM to learn WHY Godly choices are critical. You also learn HOW to practically apply your understanding to make Godly choices. The Holy Spirit uses the Word of God and His supernatural ability to give you Godly wisdom and understanding.

Let the Holy Spirit enable you with His wisdom and His understanding.

Look to no one else but the Spirit of the Lord.

CHAPTER 13

PERSONAL

NOTES

CHAPTER 14

THE SPIRIT

OF

COUNSEL

AND

POWER

Let us now look at the second pair of branches that teach us the HOW of taking God's direction and translating that into personal application to get to the end state that God wants for us.

Christians will read the Bible and understand its principles. They will know what God wants for them in their life and the right choices they have to make to get there. They will even teach those principles either in Sunday school, or in counseling sessions or even from the pulpit. But they neglect due diligence when it comes to putting those principles into effective personal application. Just having wisdom and understanding is useless because it has not done anything effective in your life other than showing you what the right choices are to get to your end state. Without the counsel and power of the Holy Spirit, a believer is incapable of reaching that high goal of conforming to the Holy One.

As an assistant pastor, I have had many opportunities to counsel people. They come to me with as small a problem as dealing with a disciplined life to as big a problem as a failing marriage. What they look for is my understanding of their problem, its seriousness, Godly advice to fix the problem and at times, an investment on my part to help them get there. The Holy Spirit is ready to do a whole lot more than that for the believer if one is truly serious about taking counsel. You might think that there is no one that understands what you are going through. On the contrary there is one.

> Seeing then that we have a great High Priest who has passed through the heavens, Jesus the Son of God, let us hold fast our confession. For we do not have a High Priest who cannot sympathize with our weaknesses, but was in all points tempted as we are, yet without sin. Let us therefore come boldly to the throne of grace, that we may obtain mercy and find grace to help in time of need. (Hebrews 4:14-16)

Jesus Christ is fully aware of your situation and your weaknesses. He knows and He sympathizes with you, and He will not allow you to fail, if you look to Him for help.

When Jesus was on earth, He told His disciples He would ask the Father for *another* helper, not just a helper.

> "If you love Me, keep My commandments. And I will pray the Father, and He will give you another Helper, that He may abide with you forever — the Spirit of truth, whom the world cannot receive, because it neither sees Him nor knows Him; but you know Him, for He dwells with you and will be in you." (John 14:15-17)

Our High Priest, Jesus Christ, says this helper will be just like

Him, with the same counsel and the same power He has. The Holy Spirit will take what Jesus knows and make it known to us.

> However, when He, the Spirit of truth, has come, He will guide you into all truth; for He will not speak on His own authority, but whatever He hears He will speak; and He will tell you things to come. He will glorify Me, for He will take of what is Mine and declare it to you. All things that the Father has are Mine. Therefore I said that He will take of Mine and declare it to you. (John 16:13-15)

The Holy Spirit has the same knowledge of you as Jesus, our High Priest, has. He can also sympathize with you just like Jesus can. Hence He knows what you need and can make that available to you.

The greatest counsel a believer can receive is directly from Jesus Christ through His Holy Spirit. How sad it is when many believers will spend so much time reading books about God, about the Bible, about Jesus Christ that people have written, but do not have the time to read the book about Jesus Christ that His Holy Spirit wrote. Your spiritual counsel must come primarily from the Word of God.

All the counsel and advice needed for a Christian to live a Godly life is in the Bible. Not only is the Bible available to us, but Jesus Christ so sympathized with our weaknesses that He also sent us a Counselor. The Holy Spirit, as the Counselor, can not only understand my weakness but can also see into my heart. He knows exactly where the problem is and has all the spiritual equipment to execute the precise surgical procedure needed to fix the problem. Unfortunately there is no spiritual anesthesia for this spiritual surgery. Instead, He supernaturally gives us the power and strength to endure it. Once the surgery is done, He continues to stay with us and nurse us back to health. He replenishes our strength and empowers us to overcome future spiritual sickness.

This submission to the Spirit, to be led by Him every second of your life is what is called "being filled with the Spirit."

> And do not be drunk with wine, in which is dissipation; but be filled with the Spirit. (Ephesians 5:18)

Many think this means we need more of the Holy Spirit. The verse actually refers to submitting oneself increasingly to the counsel of the Spirit. Some wait for that special experience of being filled with the Spirit. This is the problem that many Christians face today. They have the knowledge and the wisdom provided by the Spirit through the Word of God. But they are not willing to submit to the counsel provided by the Spirit. This is a change from following what we naturally do to a state of yielding to the Holy Spirit and doing something supernatural. It becomes even harder because this change is so radical in nature that it is like day and night, like light and darkness. But you need to believe that this change is possible because not only does the Holy Spirit provide counsel, He also provides the power to follow through.

For those who diligently read the Bible every day, you already know what the Holy Spirit's counsel is for almost all areas of your life because it is already documented in the Bible. For example, you don't need the Spirit's guidance on whether you should read your Bible today or not. That is already commanded in the Bible. You don't need to ask the Holy Spirit if you should buy that fancy car when you know you can't make your payments each month. The Scriptures are very clear warning us against going into debt. So you may wonder what counsel you really need to seek from the Spirit.

So let us take a closer look at what is involved in seeking counsel from the Spirit. Every decision or choice you make is critical in this process of letting the Holy Spirit control your life. The most important step is that you first pray and ask God to show you through His Spirit what His counsel is. This requires faith on your part to acknowledge that what God reveals to you through His Word is from God and is in your best interest.

You may already know the answer to some of your daily choices. To ensure compliance with the Word of God, you ask the Holy Spirit to confirm your decision through the Word. As you have your daily QT, He will lead you to one or several scriptures that will either confirm your choice or will show you a different path.

For those choices that are personal and specific to your life, and you don't have an answer, you need to come with an open heart and open mind. Let me illustrate with an example. In today's world, one naturally finds his or her spouse through the dating game. They date until they find the one they like and are compatible with and then come to God and seek His counsel. In a situation like this where hearts have already been joined together, rarely would one accept the Holy Spirit's counsel to stop dating that particular person. An open mind and a commitment to follow the Spirit's counsel is essential. Remember that the Spirit does have the ability to see inside your heart.

> I, the Lord, search the heart, I test the mind, Even to give every man according to his ways, According to the fruit of his doings. (Jeremiah 17:10)

God already knows if you have come with a pre-determined answer. He also knows if you are willing to submit to His counsel or not.

If you do come with a true desire to follow the Spirit's counsel, use the following filtering process to determine what His direction is.

a.) How will my decision affect my personal relationship with the Lord? Will it bring me closer and enhance it? Will it allow me to see God's power in my life? Will my actions glorify Him?

b.) How will my decision affect my family and my relationship with them? Will it bring my family closer to God? More specifically will it hinder their relationship with God? Will it open doors for God to enhance their personal relationship with Him? Will it bring the family closer to each other?

c.) How will my decision affect my ministry? Will it allow me to excel and invest more in His kingdom? Will it open doors for me to be more involved in the lives of the people God has brought into my life? Have I completed my current commitments to those God has brought into my life?

d.) How will my decision affect me financially? Will this decision lead me into more debt? Will this decision give me more capability to invest financially in the church and the congregation? Will I be able to bless others more with the finances that God gave me?

e.) Do I have more than one confirmation that this is God's will for me? Did God confirm this through multiple sources and/or multiple times?

f.) Do I have absolute peace in my heart regarding my decision? Philippians 4:7 talks about this peace.

The primary method that the Spirit uses to counsel us is the Word of God. So as you have your QT, be open to the Spirit's guidance. Give full opportunity to the Holy Spirit, and be sensitive to His leading. Whether at home, at work, in the coffee shop, as you drive, keep thinking of WHAT you understood, WHY it applies to your personal life, and HOW to determine if your choices are Godly or worldly. Do this on a regular basis. The changes you expect might be quick or over time, but don't give up.

As you understand His counsel and submit your life to be controlled by the Holy Spirit, He will begin the empowering process.

> 'Not by might nor by power, but by my Spirit,' Says the Lord of hosts. (Zechariah 4:6)

What our natural self with all its strength and power declined to do, the Holy Spirit will enable us to do supernaturally. This is also true even in cases of addiction. Perhaps you are struggling with serious additions like drugs, alcohol or pornography. Maybe you are struggling with issues like greed, gossip and anger. When the believer is willing to be driven by the Word and led by the Holy Spirit, supernatural changes are promised in the Scriptures.

> But you shall receive power when the Holy Spirit has come upon you; and you shall be witnesses to Me in Jerusalem, and in all Judea and Samaria, and to the end of the earth. (Acts 1:8)

You and I have received the Holy Spirit and He indwells in us. Jesus Christ promised that we will have His power when He has *come upon us*. This means He has complete control of our lives when we yield to His direction.

Unless you are convinced and have faith that this change is possible through the Spirit's power, you will not make any progress. By yielding to the Holy Spirit and depending on His power to overcome the world, persevere in applying His counsel to every aspect of your life.

Here is the relationship between these two enablers (counsel and power) from the Holy Spirit and your study of the Word of God.

JOSHUA 1:8	ISAIAH 11:2	YOU LEARN
MEDITATE	COUNSEL	HOW
DO	POWER	APPLICATION

When you MEDITATE on the Word of God, the Holy Spirit will COUNSEL you on how to make the right choices in every aspect of your life. When you make a commitment to DO it, the Holy Spirit will give you the POWER to APPLY what you have learned through MEDITATION. Again, the Holy Spirit uses the Word of God and His supernatural ability to give us Godly counsel and power.

Let the Holy Spirit enable you with His counsel and His power.

Look to no one else but the Spirit of the Lord.

CHAPTER 14

PERSONAL

NOTES

CHAPTER 15

THE SPIRIT

OF

KNOWLEDGE

AND

FEAR OF GOD

Now we come to the third pair of branches in the candlestick that teaches us how to measure our progress in this supernatural transformation. As we take WHAT we learn and APPLY it in our lives, we need to assess our progress. Lack of progress is an indication of a lack of commitment and motivation.

> The fear of the Lord is the beginning of wisdom, And the knowledge of the Holy One is understanding. (Proverbs 9:10)

For you to make progress in your walk with the Lord, you need motivation in addition to knowing what you need to do. You need a healthy fear of the Lord that will drive your passion for God over the edge. This fear is a combination of awe for who God is along with a fear of facing God's discipline. This fear can also be understood as a combination of reverence for God's sovereignty and a fear that is holy and humble. The purpose of this fear is to draw us to a loving God and motivate us to obey Him.

As you begin to see the wonderful transformation being accomplished by the Word of God and the Holy Spirit, you will begin to gain a true knowledge of who God is. You will begin to stand in awe of God. You will see His unconditional love, His forgiving nature, His patient encouragement, His Holiness, His sovereignty, His intimate knowledge of you, and His power over the entire world. The more you know of God, the better you understand the standard that you are being transformed to.

> That Christ may dwell in your hearts through faith; that you, being rooted and grounded in love, may be able to comprehend with all the saints what is the width and length and depth and height — to know the love of Christ which passes knowledge; that you may be filled with all the fullness of God. (Ephesians 3:17-19)

Because of this healthy fear of the Lord, you will begin to take WHAT you must do, having understood WHY and HOW to do it, and will APPLY it in your personal life. You will begin to see progress in areas of your life that you thought were impossible to change. But progress needs to be measured so you can see for yourself how the Holy Spirit supernaturally transforms your life.

You need a standard to measure your progress. This standard is none other than our Lord Jesus Christ.

> Therefore be imitators of God as dear children. And walk in love, as Christ also has loved us and given Himself for us, an offering and a sacrifice to God for a sweet-smelling aroma. (Ephesians 5:1-2)

We are called to a life of holiness by persevering to imitate God who has been revealed to us through Jesus Christ. Ephesians 5 continues to give us the knowledge of what it means to imitate Jesus Christ by following His example of love. We cannot follow His example unless we move away from our past life of darkness to this transformed life of light. The chapter continues to encourage us to be diligent and understand what the Lord's will is for our lives. We saw in the previous chapter how the Holy Spirit of counsel shows us what God's will is for our lives as we learn to yield to His leading. But how do we know we are on the right track?

Churches today are miserably failing to teach this standard of Jesus Christ due to fear of losing the congregation. Pastors are afraid to challenge believers to a life of holiness. They are afraid to confront believers when they don't measure up to the standard. This crowd-pleasing teaching only makes a believer stumble and eventually results in a couch potato believer, watching, knowing, understanding, trying, but ultimately giving up.

The believer must look to the Holy Spirit for knowledge of the Holy One, in order to measure progress tested against the life of Jesus Christ. The entire Bible is a testimony of Jesus Christ, starting with prophesies in the Old Testament, His life on earth as a human being and finally as He sits at the right hand of God as our advocate.

To imitate God means to imitate Christ in every aspect of our life, not just in those that are convenient for us. This, again, requires a diligent study of the Scriptures to understand the character of God through the life of Jesus Christ. Below are some characteristics of Jesus Christ. As you study the Bible you will come across numerous others that you must take note of so you understand the standard that you are being measured against.

- Jesus Christ was without sin. (Hebrews 4:15)
- Jesus Christ used the Word of God to overcome sin. (Matthew 4:1-10)
- Jesus Christ was full of compassion. (Matthew 15:32)
- Jesus demonstrated His unconditional love for us on the cross. (Ephesians 2:4-9)
- Jesus was baptized. (Mark 1:9-11)
- Jesus went off to a quiet place, early in the morning, to spend time in prayer. (Mark 1:35)
- Jesus came to seek and save the lost. (Luke 19:10)
- Jesus was forgiving. (John 8:10-11, Luke 23:34)
- Jesus demonstrated His humility by washing the disciples' feet. (John 18:3-5)
- Jesus came to seek and save the lost. (Luke 19:10)

This standard of Jesus Christ can never be lowered. As you gain increased knowledge of Jesus Christ, you learn to be awed at His amazing lifestyle. Through the supernatural leading of the Holy Spirit, this awe transforms into a sincere reverence for God and His power and what He has done and is able to do through His Son Jesus Christ. At the same time you will realize that God does not take sin lightly. He is quick to lovingly discipline us and get us back on track. This combination of awe and fear is what the Scriptures refer to as the fear of the Lord. It is not the "God will strike me with lightening" kind of fear but a sincere reverence and humble submission to Christ. This awe will compel you to strive even more to apply biblical principles into every aspect of your life. The desire that was just a tiny spark has now become an intense passion to imitate Jesus Christ. This passion, driven by the Word of God, enables you to submit to the leading of the Holy Spirit bringing out the transformation from darkness into light.

> By knowledge the rooms are filled with all precious and pleasant riches. (Proverbs 24:4)

As you compare your own spiritual status of the transformation with the standard of Christ, you can begin to see how much progress you have made. You will see that those things of the darkness are no longer pleasing to you anymore. The very desire for the things of the world has been lessened as you begin to put on the holy nature of Christ. Your heart has supernaturally developed an intense desire and passion for the things of the Lord.

> If then you were raised with Christ, seek those things which are above, where Christ is, sitting at the right hand of God. Set your mind on things above, not on things on the earth. For you died, and your life is hidden with Christ in God. When Christ who is our life appears, then you also will appear with Him in glory. (Colossians 3:1-4)

Here is the relationship between these two enablers (knowledge and the fear of the Lord) from the Holy Spirit and your study of the Word of God.

JOSHUA 1:8	ISAIAH 11:2	YOU LEARN
READ	KNOWLEDGE	WHAT
DO	FEAR OF THE LORD	APPLICATION

When you READ the Word of God, the Holy Spirit will give you the KNOWLEDGE to learn WHAT GOD wants for your life. When you make a commitment to DO it, the Holy Spirit will give you the fear of the Lord to diligently APPLY what you have learned through READING. The Holy Spirit uses the Word of God and His supernatural ability to give you Godly knowledge and the fear of the Lord.

Let the Holy Spirit enable you with His knowledge and His fear of the Lord.

Look to no one else but the Spirit of the Lord.

CHAPTER 15

PERSONAL

NOTES

CHAPTER 16

SPIRIT LED

Life is full of choices. Every day you make hundreds of decisions, some deliberately and some as a matter of habit. Every decision you make has a consequence associated with it. Note that these consequences many times impact future generations to come and at times, with disastrous implications.

So it is with a deliberate and diligent purpose we must submit our lives to the leading of the Holy Spirit. Speaking to a large audience, D.L. Moody held up a glass and asked, "How can I get the air out of this glass?" One man shouted, "Suck it out with a pump!" Moody replied, "That would create a vacuum and shatter the glass." After numerous other suggestions Moody smiled, picked up a pitcher of water, and filled the glass. "There," he said, "all the air is now removed." He then went on to explain that victory in the Christian life is not accomplished by "sucking out a sin here and there," but by being filled with the Holy Spirit.

> And do not be drunk with wine, in which is dissipation; but be filled with the Spirit. (Ephesians 5:18)

So what does being filled with the Holy Spirit mean? I believe there is no difference between "filled with the Spirit" and "led by the Spirit." Both mean that you are willingly controlled by the Holy Spirit. As part of the cleaning and transformation process, the Holy Spirit performs spiritual surgery in the heart. Yes, we all know that surgery is painful but there is no spiritual anesthesia for this surgery. There is only the hope that this spiritual surgery yields a better heart that is pleasing to Christ when He returns. But for the Holy Spirit to perform this cleansing spiritual surgery, one must be willing to go under His spiritual knife. To experience the true Father-son relationship through Jesus Christ, one must develop a natural habit of being obedient to (filled by) the Holy Spirit.

> For as many as are led by the Spirit of God, these are sons of God. (Romans 8:14)

Being filled with the Spirit means –
  a.) Having a spiritual perspective in everything pertaining to life.
  b.) Being subject to the direction and guidance of the Holy Spirit.

It is only when we submit to the direction, the guidance, the admonition, and the constraints of the Holy Spirit, can we expect to see any change in our hearts. Many want this change, but they want it without submission or any pain. It is so unfortunate that many believers, although they have the indwelling presence of the Holy Spirit, are not willing to experience the transforming power of the Holy Spirit.

But you ask, "How do I know that the Spirit is working in me?" Believe it or not, although you don't see the Holy Spirit work in you, you will most definitely see the results of His work.

> The wind blows where it wishes, and you hear the sound of it, but cannot tell where it comes from and where it goes. So is everyone who is born of the Spirit. (John 3:8)

Just because you don't see the Spirit, does not mean that He is not cleaning up your heart. You will see the results in the fruit of the Spirit, but only when you obey Him. You will be amazed at the change as you compare your past life to your life after you submit to the Holy Spirit. The changes in your personal life are the only evidences that you can see of the work that the Holy Spirit has done in your heart.

> But the fruit of the Spirit is love, joy, peace, longsuffering, kindness, goodness, faithfulness, gentleness, self-control. Against such there is no law. And those who are Christ's have crucified the flesh with its passions and desires. If we live in the Spirit, let us also walk in the Spirit. (Galatians 5:22-25)

Being led by the Holy Spirit does not happen without being driven by the Word of God according to Joshua 1:8. We discussed this in Chapter 10. As we READ, MEDITATE and APPLY the Word of God, the Holy Spirit through His knowledge, wisdom, counsel, understanding, power and fear of the Lord will supernaturally bring about His fruit to blossom in your life.

As you READ the Word of God, the Holy Spirit enables us through KNOWLEDGE and UNDERSTANDING to clearly determine WHAT God requires of us.

As you MEDITATE on the Word of God, the Holy Spirit

enables us through WISDOM and COUNSEL to clearly determine WHY we have to obey God and HOW we can practically apply it in our lives.

As you DO (obey) the Word of God, the Holy Spirit enables us through POWER and FEAR to successfully APPLY biblical principles in every aspect of our lives.

As you see this fruit develop in your life, your awe of God compels you to continue to persevere in your walk. The very fact that you have made progress will encourage you and tremendously increase your faith in the Word of God and the Holy Spirit's Guidance. Your passion and delight for the Word will increase, thereby increasing your willingness to yield to the Holy Spirit. All of this brings about this amazing supernatural transformation into the image of God, preparing you for Christ's return. No one knows when Christ will return, not even Jesus Christ. Only the Father knows when it is time for the wedding. You and I should be ready for this return of Jesus Christ. So let the Holy Spirit be your counselor and yield to Him as He prepares you for Christ's return.

As this process continues, the believer's heart is being cleansed and is evidenced by the daily demonstration of the fruit of the Spirit. You will see this evidence in your personal walk with the Lord, in your marriage, in your relationship with your children, in your ministry, in your work, in your response to stressful situations, in your ability to forgive the offender, in your ability to love your enemy and in many other areas of your life. As your heart becomes pure, you begin to see clearly who God really is.

> Blessed are the pure in heart, For they shall see God. (Matthew 5:8)

How cool is it that you can actually have a glimpse or even more, of who God is. You can see what His character is and how the heart of a once-upon-a-time sinner can actually connect with the holiest of holies. It is an unbelievable experience. It is like an addition to a drug. You are now convinced that without that daily connection with God through Jesus Christ, His Word and the power of the Holy Spirit, you would not want to live anymore. Life without that deep and intense relationship with Jesus Christ is not worth living. Every believer must come to this state of total dependence on Jesus Christ through God's Spirit.

I urge you to completely yield to the Holy Spirit and depend on His enablers in every aspect of your life. Only then will your life be *Spirit Led.*

CHAPTER 16

PERSONAL

NOTES

CHAPTER 17

WORD DRIVEN

SPIRIT LED

So far, we discussed the power of God's Word and of the Holy Spirit. In this chapter, I want to show you the connection between the work that God's Word does and the work that the Holy Spirit does. Without the illumination given by the Holy Spirit, the Word of God is difficult to understand and apply. Let me summarize the relationship between the Word of God and the Holy Spirit.

JOSHUA 1:8	PSALM 19:7,8	ISAIAH 11:2	YOU LEARN
READ	PURE	UNDERSTANDING & KNOWLEDGE	WHAT
MEDITATE	SURE	WISDOM & COUNSEL	WHY/HOW
DO	RIGHT/PERFECT	POWER & FEAR OF THE LORD	APPLICATION

As you read the Word of God because it is pure, the Holy Spirit will give you knowledge and understanding to learn what God requires of you.

As you meditate on the Word of the God because it is sure, the Holy Spirit will give you wisdom and counsel to understand why you have to follow the Bible and how to practically apply it in your life.

As you follow (do) the Word of God because it is perfect and right, the Holy Spirit will give you power and fear of the Lord to diligently apply biblical principles in every area of your life.

You must let God's Word and the enablers of the Holy Spirit control every aspect of your life. You will then start to see a supernatural transformation happening in the very core of your heart.

Galatians 5 describes this transformation, but I do want to caution you that it does not happen overnight. Just because a sinner is born again does not necessarily mean that a switch is turned on and change happens. A switch is indeed turned on and the tiniest of sparks with a desire to change is fired up. This spark must be kept aflame so that the desire turns into a passion resulting in an uncompromising commitment to holiness.

A change includes a previous state and a new state. Let us look at the previous state of a Christian. Mind you that this state might be that of a person before being born again or sometimes even after being born again.

> Now the works of the flesh are evident, which are: adultery, fornication, uncleanness, lewdness, idolatry, sorcery, hatred, contentions, jealousies, outbursts of wrath, selfish ambitions, dissensions, heresies, envy, murders, drunkenness, revelries, and the like; of which I tell you beforehand, just as I also told you in time past, that those who practice such things will not inherit the kingdom of God. (Galatians 5:19-21)

The above verses describe what the Scriptures call the *works of the flesh*. This is what our flesh automatically desires to do.

The flesh includes all our senses, even our emotions and feelings. What the flesh causes us to do always makes us feel good, although only temporarily. The new state is evidenced by the *fruit of the Spirit*.

> But the fruit of the Spirit is love, joy, peace, longsuffering, kindness, goodness, faithfulness, gentleness, self-control. Against such there is no law. And those who are Christ's have crucified the flesh with its passions and desires. If we live in the Spirit, let us also walk in the Spirit. (Galatians 5: 22-25)

From a human change perspective we call this a paradigm shift. You see, before a person is born again, it is natural for a person to do what the flesh desires. Now that one is born again and has the Spirit indwelling in the heart, he or she has to be sensitive to the leading of the Spirit.

What comes naturally must now be run past the Holy Spirit for a determination of whether that action is now acceptable to God or not. That is a dramatic change. No longer can one depend on feelings or emotions or logic or what makes sense. There are now two checks that must be performed before acting on a decision. One must check with the conscience (in our mind) and then go a step further to filter it through the convictions of the heart. One must now follow this new determination process without fully understanding it or knowing what the consequences will be, but just trusting that both the mind and the heart are in agreement.

Only a confirmed alignment of the mind with the heart results in a decision that pleases God. In human terms, that is a radical change, from being dependant on self (emotions, feelings, a seared conscience and a wicked heart) to placing our dependence on Christ (*Word driven* mind and a *Spirit led* heart).

The Holy Spirit now indwells in our lives as a reminder and a guarantee that a change is now possible and will occur if we are led by the Spirit. By submitting to the indwelling nature of the Holy Spirit, every Christian is given a chance to acquire wisdom, understanding, counsel, power, knowledge, and live in the fear of the Lord. It is only when a person submits to the Holy Spirit that he or she sees the powerful, life-changing impact of the Word of God. The Holy Spirit is ready to teach. Will you submit and listen? If you don't, then you are, by default, listening to the world.

Now that the Spirit is working on the heart, one might believe that life is good. The problem is we have this thing called mind having a conscience that might have been seared. When the mind processes its decisions and realizes that the output of the mind is not in alignment with the heart, it goes into *chaos* mode. At that time, anything can happen and Christians are prone to make spiritually irrational decisions. They take chances, sometimes incorrectly assured that what they are doing is actually right in God's sight. So how do we align our mind with the heart? Let us review Romans 12:1-2 again.

> I beseech you therefore, brethren, by the mercies of God, that you present your bodies a living sacrifice, holy, acceptable to God, which is your reasonable service. And do not be conformed to this world, but be transformed by the renewing of your mind, that

you may prove what is that good and acceptable and perfect will of God. (Romans 12:1-2)

We have to renew the mind by erasing the ideas and the knowledge of good and evil that was burned into our conscience during our sinful life and then reprogramming it with a new knowledge of good and evil. This reprogramming must be driven by the Word of God that has the right definition of what is good and evil. This knowledge must remain burned into our conscience, un-erasable by any kind of worldly reasoning or wisdom. Here is a list of some of the truths that I have reprogrammed into my mind.

a.) God is in sovereign control of my life. Not that I see it but I believe it. (Matthew 6:25-34)

b.) Sometimes things go wrong in my life, but God has the power to change them for my own good. (Romans 8:28)

c.) I have the power to say NO to any temptation. If I give in, it is only because I have chosen to do so. (1 Corinthians 10:13, Romans 6:11)

d.) Divorce is not an option. God, through this Word and His Spirit, has the power to reconcile any marriage that submits to His direction, even if adultery is involved. (Malachi 2:16, 1 Corinthians 7:10,11,27)

There are many more truths I can list, but you get the idea. Every one of the above convictions have been imprinted in my mind and cannot be erased or proven false. Even if there is adequate evidence that one is false, I won't accept it because it contradicts the Word of God. This list I have in my mind now has become my new set of ground rules during every decision making process that my mind and heart go through.

To come to that form of an unshakeable conviction, one must align the mind to the convictions that occur in the heart. Joshua 1:8 and Psalms 119:9,11 describe the process of this alignment.

The process described in Joshua 1:8 is a repetitive process. I call it the RMD process – Read, Meditate and Do. This RMD process must happen 24/7 each day. Let me explain. In Chapter 10, I described to you what Quiet Time (QT) is for a Christian. Assuming you are having your QT every day, you read the Bible during that time. You also meditate or think about what God is saying to you through the portion you read. Then you see how that applies specifically to your life. Finally you take action to practically implement learned concepts in your personal life.

Now Psalms 119:11 says that when a person hides God's Word in his heart, he now has the ability to overcome sin. So during your QT, when you meditate on the Word, you realize that God is teaching you something important, so you commit that scripture to memory. This is what I described in Chapter 10 as scripture memory. So adding memorization to RMD, I will change the acronym to RMMD – Read, Meditate, Memorize and Do. This RMMD cycle is what renews your mind to be in alignment with the convictions that happen in your heart. But you also have to assess your performance daily to see if your life is in compliance with the Word of God.

For if anyone is a hearer of the word and not a doer,

he is like a man observing his natural face in a mirror; for he observes himself, goes away, and immediately forgets what kind of man he was. But he who looks into the perfect law of liberty and continues in it, and is not a forgetful hearer but a doer of the work, this one will be blessed in what he does. (James 1:23-25)

So not only do you RMMD, you also need to assess your progress based on the standard of Christ. Let me add this to the RMMD process to finalize the acronym to RMMDA – Read, Meditate, Memorize, Do, and Assess.

When the mind is renewed by the Word of God and the heart is convicted by the Holy Spirit, the outcome is a perfect alignment of the mind and heart that allows you to see Jesus Christ as your master. Such an alignment causes an uncompromising commitment to Jesus and rewrites the doctrines and the ground rules that now govern your life.

What is the evidence of this transformation? You see it when you come to the point when obeying God is not a chore anymore but really a pleasure. No longer is it "Do I have to?" but now it is always "I want to".

It is by being *Word Driven* and *Spirit Led* that you prepare yourself for the return of the Lord.

CHAPTER 17

PERSONAL

NOTES

CHAPTER 18

CONCLUSION

Based on the scriptures we reviewed and the simple principles I have presented, I trust you have come to realize that living a victorious life is not really a burdensome chore. God gave us two powerful persons, the Word personified in Jesus Christ and the Holy Spirit, to help us, guide us and work an incredible transformation in our lives. It is our responsibility to depend on the Word and the Holy Spirit. Without this complete dependence, our transformation would be difficult or even impossible.

Dear saint, the transformation is not a result of fighting sin every day which is a losing battle. It has to be a result of you being driven by the Word and led by the Holy Spirit. Let the Word permeate every ounce of your spiritual body, and submit completely to the Holy Spirit. Being filled with the Holy Spirit is more a measure of how much you submit to the Holy Spirit rather than having more of the Spirit in your life.

Your daily life must be overwhelmed with the Word, making every decision that conforms to the Scriptures. You must practically apply what the Word commands you to do. For this to happen, your mind has to be reprogrammed so that the filter you use to make your daily choices is specifically the Word of God. Not some book or idea or a neat philosophy that you picked up somewhere. Be careful that you are not deceived by doctrines that mimic the Scriptures. Do not depend on what you feel in your heart. Sometimes, the strongest feelings in your heart are your greatest enemy. Being driven by God's Word is a predecessor to being led by the Holy Spirit.

Unless your mind has been reprogrammed by God's Word, the Holy Spirit's work on the heart would not give you the strength you need to follow through on your commitments. The mind must agree with the heart for biblical action to take place. Unless the mind is renewed by being *Word driven* and the heart is convicted by being *Spirit Led*, biblical action is only an idea. It is absolutely, imperatively, necessary that both – the renewing of the mind and the conviction in the heart - must happen simultaneously. Many will ignore the diligence required to be driven by God's Word, but rather expect the Holy Spirit to miraculously change their lives. This transformation is a continuous salvation from the power of sin that is accomplished only by an uncompromising partnership with our Lord Jesus Christ.

As your mind is being renewed, the Holy Spirit changes and convicts the heart bringing the mind and the heart into alignment. Once that alignment happens, the natural result is the ability to follow through on the practical implementation of God's direction in your life. The effort by the believer in renewing the mind, combined with the life changing work of the Holy Spirit in the believer's heart brings about the automatic, supernatural transformation that God has promised us in the Scriptures.

Be driven by God's Word and be led by the Holy Spirit, and the Bible guarantees that your life will be changed.

May the Lord Jesus himself walk you through this

transformation. See for yourself this wonderful and marvelous process. Build an uncompromising relationship with Jesus Christ by being *Word driven* and *Spirit led*.

May God accomplish in you what He has started to do when he found you, saved you and adopted you into His family.

> I thank my God upon every remembrance of you, always in every prayer of mine making request for you all with joy, for your fellowship in the gospel from the first day until now, being confident of this very thing, that He who has begun a good work in you will complete it until the day of Jesus Christ. (Philippians 1:3-6)

My prayer for you is that you are *Word driven* and *Spirit led*.

God bless you.

CHAPTER 18

PERSONAL

NOTES